at this moment: the story of
michael bublé

at this moment: the story of
michael bublé

michael heatley

OMNIBUS PRESS
London / New York / Paris / Sydney / Copenhagen / Berlin / Madrid / Tokyo

Copyright © 2011 Omnibus Press
(A Division of Music Sales Limited)

Cover designed by Fresh Lemon
Picture research by Jacqui Black

ISBN: 978.1.84938.978.5
Order No: OP54021

The Author hereby asserts his/her right to be identified as the author of this work in accordance with Sections 77 to 78 of the Copyright, Designs and Patents Act 1988.

All rights reserved. No part of this book may be reproduced in any form or by any electronic or mechanical means, including information storage or retrieval systems, without permission in writing from the publisher, except by a reviewer who may quote brief passages.

Exclusive Distributors
Music Sales Limited,
14/15 Berners Street,
London, W1T 3LJ.

Music Sales Corporation,
257 Park Avenue South,
New York, NY 10010, USA.

Macmillan Distribution Services,
56 Parkwest Drive
Derrimut, Vic 3030,
Australia.

Every effort has been made to trace the copyright holders of the photographs in this book but one or two were unreachable. We would be grateful if the photographers concerned would contact us.

The author would like to thank Graham Betts, Mike Gent and Drew Heatley for their invaluable assistance.

Typeset by Phoenix Photosetting, Chatham, Kent

Printed in the EU

A catalogue record for this book is available from the British Library.

Visit Omnibus Press on the web at www.omnibuspress.com

Contents

Introduction		vii
Chapter 1:	Early Life	1
Chapter 2:	The Struggling Years	22
Chapter 3:	The First LP	42
Chapter 4:	It's Time	67
Chapter 5:	Call Me Irresponsible	90
Chapter 6:	Crazy Love	112
Chapter 7:	Away From The Spotlight	135
Chapter 8:	The Future	156
Discography		171

Introduction

Luck, marketing, talent. Three ingredients for success that are as crucial today as they have ever been. Michael Bublé, the besuited Canadian who rose to worldwide fame in the second half of the millennium's first decade, has been blessed with all three.

Even his critics must admit that Bublé has carved a niche for himself as an entertainer who can fill arenas anywhere from Manchester to Manila. But those who pigeonhole him as a middle-of-the-road performer with a totally female audience seduced by his looks are wide of the mark. Sales figures for each album that run into the millions and a mixed-sex live audience suggest his appeal is somewhat wider.

His style of audience interaction is both edgy and humorous, not to mention self-deprecating. Having announced his engagement to a British crowd in 2010, he managed to defuse any feelings of resentment from his female fans by putting his own sexuality into question. "Half of you just booed me," he laughed, "and all the men just turned to their wives and girlfriends and said 'Oh he is *so* gay, please!' If that were true, I'd tell the whole world about it. And [points to man in front row] I would bonk you in two seconds, Mr Sweater Man…"

So what does it take to become a success in the 21st century? Not a great deal, if shows like *The X Factor* are any guide. Catch the eye of a Simon Cowell or a Cheryl Cole and you too can enjoy 15 minutes of fame at the drop of a hat. Yet even a performer who has paid their dues, to use the old cliché, needs some help along the way. And there's no doubt that the story of Michael Bublé's discovery reads more like fiction than fact. He was spotted by mega-producer David Foster – who has worked with everyone from Michael Jackson and Paul McCartney to Mariah Carey and Celine Dion – singing at the Canadian prime minister's wedding – an unlikely story that Michael now tells against himself.

But Bublé was far from an overnight sensation. He had worked the clubs, starred in musicals, delivered singing telegrams and even strolled the shopping malls of his native Canada dressed as Santa Claus. The fisherman's son from British Columbia had stood out at school for preferring Tony Bennett to Bon Jovi, but it took time for him to catch a wave to success.

Call Michael Bublé middle of the road and he'll laugh all the way to the bank. There's no doubt that his management are savvy enough to milk all the appropriate sources of revenue that help to keep the star on the world's biggest stages. In 2010, for instance, he teamed up with Napa Valley-based Beringer Vineyards, who became the 'official wine' of 2010's Crazy Love Tour. "The exclusive partnership," the press release gushed, "will include valuable offers and experiences for Bublé fans at numerous retail, restaurant and concert venues. The collaboration will also include unique online components throughout the duration of the tour."

What all this has to do with music is open to debate. But these days it's as much the lifestyle you buy into as the music. Which is ironic, since Bublé rejects his perceived lounge-lizard persona. "You know it's funny, I don't personally live the lifestyle. I don't wear a fedora and I don't sit at the bar and have a Martini and I don't smoke cigars,

Introduction

but the music to me was just so powerful. It was just impossible to get away from." Not so much Ol' Blue Eyes, more an ordinary Joe...

Many of the trappings of fame sit uneasily with a man who, given a brand-new, top-of-the-range convertible BMW after he agreed to be photographed for an advertisement, gave it back within a week and a half. "It was too ostentatious for me," he explained, adding, "I've never had so many people give me the finger driving a car! And I got pulled over twice by the cops..." Not bad for someone who, five years or so before, couldn't get arrested!

The dividing line between middle-of-the-road predictability and the retro-cool Bublé exudes is narrow but crucial. Frank Sinatra was a role model, but maybe a better parallel would be Norah Jones. Like Michael, she spoke to generations disenfranchised by MTV, and her breakthrough in 2002 was a morale boost as our man prepared to take on the might of the multinational labels.

Now Bublé, a Warner Brothers recording artist, is the man with might on his side. He has the same producer as Celine Dion, the same manager as Bryan Adams and the same publicist as Madonna. In fact, when Madonna left Warners for Live Nation in 2007, Bublé became the biggest solo star in the company's music family.

The benchmark for Canadian artists in the worldwide entertainment business had been set by Celine Dion in the previous decade. Given that Michael spoke English as his mother tongue, it seemed his path to global fame might be even easier. But his first ten years as a recording artist coincided with the decline and fall of the music business as it had existed for the previous 40 years. The switch to the digital format in the shape of compact discs had been followed by the virtual abolition of the CD in favour of downloads.

There was no indication, however, that Bublé's audience as a whole was ready to relinquish physical product. Indeed, he successfully employed a Special Edition strategy, reissuing a current album with a bonus disc containing otherwise unavailable tracks, at least one of which would have become a hit since the album first appeared. This, of course, came to be a crucial purchase for fans, as well as attracting those to whom the hit had appealed.

Another strand in the Bublé strategy would be using the DVD format to present him visually as well as aurally. The successor to the video would prove profitable, and these releases showcasing his easy mastery of the stage would win him Grammy Awards as well as fans.

And when, in 2007, Michael made it in Britain, where earlier crooner Harry Connick Jr never hit big despite repeated record-company efforts, his global success was confirmed. As an Italian-Canadian there were no blood ties to Canada's 'mother country', but he developed a rapport with British audiences that would remain unrivalled and ensure him a warm welcome on his regular return visits.

We will finish this introduction as we began it, with *The X Factor*. When Michael appeared on the UK TV programme in October 2010, he was slated for miming. In reality he had been ill and had lowered the key of the song he was performing to make sure he hit the high notes. The criticism, refutation of which actually enhanced Bublé's performing reputation, suggested that certain commentators had taken their eye off the ball.

That's something Michael Bublé has yet to do. As he looks to take ultimate creative control of his career, he is still only in his mid-thirties. The prospect of many further successful decades at the top is certainly mouth-watering, and he shows no sign of running out of inspiration, whether self-penned or derived from the Great American Songbook.

The future's bright. The future's Bublé.

CHAPTER 1

Early Life

First things first – the name. Yes, we all know by now it's pronounced *Boo-blay*, but where exactly does it come from?

Michael's maternal grandparents, Yolanda and Demetrio 'Mitch' Santagà, had emigrated to Canada from Italy. Mitch originally hailed from the village of Preganziol, 20 kilometres north-west of Venice, while Yolanda Moscone was born in Carrufo, Villa Santa Lucia degli Abruzzi, a small town in central Italy near to the Adriatic coast. On the strength of this, Bublé was able to claim dual Italian-Canadian nationality, becoming the proud owner of an Italian passport in October 2005.

Because of the name Bublé and the fact that Michael is Canadian, people often assume he is of French descent. He acknowledges that his surname "sounds French, but I'm a very proud Canadian of Italian extraction." Misunderstanding over the name's origin and pronunciation persist, as Michael laments. "I have heard Buu-lee, Bib-lee, Boo-Lee, Bubbles. Because I am Canadian, I get people who think I speak French. They just come up to me speaking French, and I have no idea what they are saying."

At This Moment: The Michael Bublé Story

When Michael's paternal great-grandparents arrived in Vancouver from Italy they were known as Bubli. The spelling was modified and the acute accent added over the 'e' to help English speakers with its pronunciation and prevent them from saying 'Bubble'. An alternative theory has it that the surname 'Buble' (that is, without the accent) is Croatian; it is based on the rumour that his father's side of the family originally came from Istria, a town close to the Croatian/Italian border.

Whatever the truth, it's certain that Michael Steven Bublé, the first child of Lewis and Amber Bublé, was born on 9 September 1975 in Burnaby, British Columbia. Part of Canada's Pacific Northwest, Burnaby lies to the east of Vancouver on the Fraser Valley, near to the border with the United States. Founded in 1892 as a rural settlement, its expansion went hand in hand with the neighbouring cities of New Westminster and Vancouver. When Michael Bublé was growing up in the Seventies and Eighties, its population was around 150,000.

The town continued to grow. It became a city in 1992 and has adapted itself to the changing economic climate, relying more on heavy industry and technology and less on the traditional activities of agriculture and logging. It now forms part of the regional district dubbed Metro Vancouver. Until Michael Bublé came along, Burnaby's most famous natives were actor Michael J Fox of *Back To The Future/Family Ties* fame, who moved to the town aged 10, and Carrie-Anne Moss, one of the stars of *The Matrix* trilogy.

Bublé's father, Lewis, was a fisherman who spent long periods each summer on his boat bound for the icy waters of Alaska, leaving housewife and mother Amber to bring up their children – Michael was soon joined by two younger sisters – with help from her own parents. The closeness of the family ties was an important factor in Michael's development, particularly his relationship with his grandfather, who introduced him to music. As his grandmother would later recall, "Michael's dad wasn't around in the summertime so the kids would come over all the time. To please his grandfather, Michael would learn these old songs. But he loved them, too, and it seemed like he would hear a song once and be able to sing it."

The elder of Michael's sisters, Brandee, became a special needs teacher and, as Brandee Ubels, mother to Michael's nephew and niece O'Shea and Jayde. "Can you believe she went from Bublé to Ubels when she got married? One funny name to another," her father commented.

The baby of the family, Crystal, followed her brother into showbusiness as an actress. She was a keen dancer as a schoolgirl but an ankle injury meant she turned her attention to acting. Crystal began her television career while still at school, appearing as Clover in four episodes of Global Television's teen drama *Madison* in 1996. This was the first of many television appearances both in Canada and the United States, the most notable being the role of Billie in the Canadian police show *Cold Squad* from 2001 to 2003.

Her movie career began as an extra in the 1996 Canadian-produced *Kissed*, followed by a small part in *Rollercoaster* (1999), a more substantial one in *Christina's House* (2000), and a starring role in 2007's *Dress To Kill* (originally entitled *Crossing*). The last-named won her a nomination for a Leo Award, given by British Columbia's film and television industry, for Best Lead Performance by a Female in a Feature Length Drama.

Lewis and Amber Bublé were staunch Roman Catholics and naturally raised their children in the faith they shared. As a child, Michael owned a white-covered Bible that he put to a particular purpose. "I used to sleep with the Bible and I'd pray every night, like, 'Please God, please God, give me a voice.'" As so often happens, however, his feelings about Catholicism were to change over the years. "I was really religious growing up… [but] now I have my own personal relationship with religion. There's certain things I didn't agree with or couldn't be more against." He was particularly struck by the discrepancy between the riches on display in Catholic churches and the poverty in the world. "We were going to these churches that were more opulent than any hotel I'd ever been in and I was thinking – now there are poor people and sick people, and, as much as l love God's house to look good, this is ridiculous."

According to his mother, Amber, Michael informed the family that he was going to be famous at the tender age of two. He first displayed his precocious singing ability when he learned his address by making a tune out of it – 'Three-Oh-Four-Eight, Car-din-al Drive'.

He was around six or seven when music made a first, and lasting, impression on him. "My first musical memory had to be listening to Bing Crosby's *White Christmas* record." A Bublé family favourite, the album (originally known as *Merry Christmas*) was a compilation of yuletide classics. Alongside the title track were carols ('Silent Night'), hymns ('Faith Of Our Fathers') and more recent festive tunes such as 'Santa Claus Is Coming To Town'. "I'd just be ecstatic because Bing Crosby's *White Christmas* would be playing in the house. I drove my parents *nuts*. Five years old and I listened to that thing through July." In other interviews he has also claimed to have "listened to that record all year".

For the young Michael, the festive season was special not so much for the giving and receiving of presents, but simply because of Crosby's album. "I just think that it was so melodic and his voice was so rich, and it's actually where I discovered, I guess, jazz, and when I hear it… it takes me right back." In the early Eighties, Crosby was at best regarded as kitsch, but Michael was oblivious to that. "It was playing all through the house and even at that young age I just thought it was the coolest stuff in the world."

Further describing the effect that the album had on him, Michael said, "Right away, as a kid, I thought that was very hip. The swing, the feel, was so attractive. As I got older I found I had an affinity for the music. I loved the instrumentation. It was really more about the style of the music. As I got older, in my early teens, my grandfather started playing everything from Frank Sinatra to Bobby Darin to Elvis Presley. I fell in love with the style of these singers, the style of the songs, the lyrics and the melody. I found all the elements almost timeless."

Michael Bublé began his formal education at the age of five, attending Seaforth Elementary School in Burnaby. He remembers it fondly as "a school that parents fought to get their kids into. It was a wonderful, sheltered cosy place with great teachers and a principal who knew everyone's name." At 11 he developed a "huge crush" on his teacher Mrs Moore, whom he described as "a strikingly beautiful woman, about 30 at the time. She was an amazing person. At that age it had an effect on me to see a woman who was so gorgeous but strong too. She was quite reserved, very classy, and I'd do anything to give Mrs Moore an apple."

Never one to forget his roots, Michael remained in contact with Seaforth and encountered Mrs Moore again when he returned to present a cheque. He was dismayed to realise that she was now nervous of *him* when he felt it should have been the other way round.

Although an urban community in its own right, Burnaby is very much a suburb of Vancouver, British Columbia's largest city, which Michael generally cites as his home town. Ice hockey, known simply as hockey in North America, occupies a similar place in Canada's sporting pantheon as football (or soccer) in England. Bublé maintains that "Vancouver is one of the greatest hockey towns in the world. I mean, who compares to us? Maybe Toronto, maybe Montreal. We're crazy about our hockey."

Michael and his father were season-ticket holders for the Vancouver Canucks, regularly travelling to the team's home fixtures at the Pacific Coliseum. In 1995, the Canucks relocated to the bigger, state-of-the art Rogers Arena where, 15 years later, Michael would finish his 2010 tour with a sellout concert.

He has vivid memories of attending the matches. "I went to every single home game as a kid and I remember those beautiful yellow jerseys everyone thought were so ugly," he said, referring to the controversial shirt design the Canucks sported between 1978 and 1985. He reels off a list of favourite players from his boyhood: "I remember I wanted to be Gary Lupul, I wanted to be Patrik Sundström and Ivan Hlinka. I used to think that being named Michael Bublé was pretty cool because I was close to being called Jiří Bubla." (Czech-born Bubla was a defensive player who played for the Canucks from 1982 to 1986.)

Michael harboured dreams of becoming a professional hockey player, playing around the home and in the street. "If you ask my dad and my mom, my hockey career started in our house and garage, where I ruined every wall because I put hockey pucks through them. I played as a kid and I think my hands were pretty good, but my skating was atrocious. I was a forward and I didn't backcheck [rushing back to defend when the other team attack]."

He waxes lyrical about the allure of the sport, with a note of regret that he was not good enough to play at the highest level. "Hockey to me is the fastest, most beautiful, intricate game there is. I love it. I love playing it, I love watching it. I eat it, I drink it." The whole ethos of the sport appealed to him. "I loved the rough and tumble of the game, the fighting. And I was OK but not good enough."

His assessment of own abilities as a player has varied over the years. "In my dreams, I wanted to be drafted by the Vancouver Canucks. I wanted so bad to be a hockey player, and the truth is that I sucked. If I was any good at hockey, I probably wouldn't be singing right now. I'd probably be sitting out the season [on the bench]."

From boyhood, Michael's life was dominated by his twin passions for music and hockey. Reflecting on the two recently, he reached a perhaps surprising conclusion. "A couple of nights ago, me and a few friends were having a few beers, and they asked me what I couldn't

Early Life

live without; and when I thought about it, sadly, I think I could live without music but I don't think I could live without hockey. I think it's the greatest game on Earth."

Born in the mid-Seventies, Bublé could have been influenced by disco or arena rock or even punk rock. He should in fact have been a paid-up member of the MTV generation. Instead his grandfather pulled out his old records and introduced Bublé to Forties – to Sixties-era singers like Frank Sinatra, Ray Charles, and Bobby Darin. His father was a fan of heavy rock, most notably Led Zeppelin and The Who. "You still playing that faggot music?" he would joke, as his son delved back into a bygone musical past.

Grandpa Mitch, as Michael calls him, played a central role in Bublé's development, and Michael has acknowledged his influence many times. "My grandfather was really my best friend growing up. He was the one who opened me up to a whole world of music that seemed to have been passed over by my generation. Although I like rock 'n' roll and modern music, the first time my grandad played me the Mills Brothers, something magical happened. The lyrics were so romantic, so real… the way a song should be for me. It was like seeing my future flash before me. I wanted to be a singer and I knew that this was the music that I wanted to sing."

The Mills Brothers were a jazz-pop vocal quartet who sold 50 million records in a career spanning from 1928 to 1970. A major influence on Dean Martin, they had fallen out of favour by the time Michael discovered them. Mitch subsequently delved deeper into his extensive record collection to introduce Michael to a roll-call of great singers from the swing era and beyond: Louis Armstrong, Ella Fitzgerald, Mel Tormé, Sarah Vaughan, Al Martino and Tony Bennett. Even Elvis Presley discs found their way onto the turntable, but Michael was not blinded by the king of rock 'n' roll. "I just *love* Elvis," he's said, "but really most of the time it was about discovering someone like Al Martino or the Mills Brothers."

By the time he had reached the age of 13 he had exposed himself to many different kinds of music, with the result that his tastes were far wider than the average teen. "My grandpa really helped ignite more of a flame. All I wanted to do was to learn more and more." It was the quality of the voices that entranced him. "Listening to Mel Tormé or Ella Fitzgerald or Frank Sinatra as a kid was so great because they had this dulcet tonal quality that I hadn't heard in modern singers."

Barely into his teens, Michael was already a devotee of swing and instinctively understood what made the music tick. "Even at that young age I thought the words were something I could understand and the melodies were so catchy. For me, that feeling of a group getting into pocket [in the groove] – and I'm not just talking about songs with vocals, just a jazz band – when they get into pocket and they're swinging, it's something that you feel through your whole body and you can't stop tapping your knee. That's pretty much what I live for, and I always did. I've always felt that way."

His assimilation of the style was even more remarkable, given that, as Michael admitted, he was born far too late to see these singers on stage. "I only listened to their music, but everything I was going to learn I pretty much learned by listening to the lifetimes' work of these artists."

Grandfather and grandson bonded not only over music but sport too, discussion ranging over who was the greatest hockey player or the greatest crooner. They spent many hours listening to vinyl records, using an old turntable to play jazz and swing music, genres that were terminally unhip. Not that this mattered to Michael. "I'm a sentimental person and the lyrics are quite sentimental. The melodies are terrific. The songs are just beautiful and I fell for them and never let them go."

His ambitions to achieve success by performing this kind of music must have seemed a highly unlikely dream. Nevertheless,

Mitch Santagà stuck firmly to the conviction that his grandson was going to resurrect the genre. Remarkably, it turned out that Michael was possessed of a singing voice ideal for the music he loved. "What if I'd fallen in love with heavy metal?" he reflected in 2004. "It was flukey. I fell in love with the music I'm suited for."

The first evidence of this happy accident came in 1988, when the family were returning from Mitch and Yolanda's annual Christmas Eve party. "I was 13 when my parents realised that I could sing. I was in the back seat of the car with my sisters. Mum and dad were driving us home from grandma and grandpa's one Christmas Eve, and we were singing carols. I think we were singing 'White Christmas', and they all stopped and I just kept singing, and everyone just turned and looked at me with their mouths open, like, 'Who's that?', and that was the first time my parents said, 'What the hell? Where did *that* come from?'" Amber Bublé also vividly recalled the incident and the family's surprise, recounting much the same anecdote from the audience during her son's appearance on the *Oprah Winfrey Show* in 2009.

Analysing the personality traits he inherited from his parents, Michael compared himself first with his mother. "We're both fiery, passionate and have quick tempers. We forgive easily, but we can get angry quickly too. My father Lewis is very mellow. I'd say the sweet side of me, that's soft and sentimental, is my dad, while the fiery, outgoing side is my mum."

Asked where his singing voice comes from, Michael was quick to credit his father. "He has a nice tone of voice, and he has a great memory but, for songs, it's unbelievably terrible. Basically, he would pick a song and he would go, 'When the moon hits your eye like a big pizza pie… When the moon hits your eye…', and he would repeat the one line a thousand times. I'd be like, 'Get it, dad – *learn* the damn song!'"

Grandpa Mitch was first struck by his grandson's vocal ability the following Christmas. "He used to sing with a broom handle as a mike. He was a born performer, a real hambone. Then, one Boxing Day, when he was about 14, he started singing 'New York, New York' with a karaoke set he got for Christmas. He floored me, I thought – this guy's really got talent."

Mitch began to compile cassettes so that Michael could listen on his Walkman personal tape player and learn the songs. Added to this was a little tongue-in-cheek emotional blackmail. "He started saying to me, 'Hey Sunshine [Mitch's nickname for him], before grandpa dies could you learn 'Stardust'?'" Michael confirmed. "It was kind of a guilt trip, but he didn't have to do much convincing." He recalls that "I'd go and learn the songs word for word, sit with him at the table and I'd sing him the song."

The pair even performed the occasional duet. "Grandpa got a real kick out of the fact that I liked the music so much. We'd start singing at the dinner table together, like 'Everybody Loves Somebody Sometime'." The musical education and influence did not operate solely in one direction, either, as Michael got to introduce Mitch to contemporary performers he loved, from Harry Connick Jr to Diana Krall.

Over 20 years later Michael would serenade his grandfather at a gig in São Paolo with his favourite song, Harry Warren and Mack Gordon's 'You'll Never Know'. But an event like that could not have seemed remotely possible in the mid-Eighties. Swing music was almost alien to Michael's generation. His devotion to it threatened to set Michael apart from his contemporaries at an age when conformity was crucial. "It was definitely not normal. But a lot of the songs speak about love and all of us can relate to that. So it wasn't *that* crazy. It's just me and how I grew up and what I thought was cool," he says. "There was always something special about that music to me. It just stood out. I always felt like I was born in the wrong time."

Early Life

When Michael turned 13, the safe haven of Seaforth Elementary was replaced by the less welcoming environment of Cariboo Hill Secondary School. Situated in a park-like suburban area, Cariboo Hill was the smallest high school in Burnaby. Michael would look back on his time there with mixed feelings, but acknowledged that the experience helped toughen him up. "I was the sweet kid. I was nice… By the time I got out of high school, I was a fighter."

He has also insisted that he was as well versed in the popular music of his adolescence as the music he grew up to sing. "It offends me when people think I only listen to Frank Sinatra. I was born in 1975 and I never wanted to be part of the Rat Pack. As a kid, my biggest idol was Michael Jackson. As a teenager, I wanted to be one of the Beastie Boys." He later expanded on this, explaining the roots of his style. "Pop had a huge influence on me, so it was important to take [jazz standards and pop] and create a hybrid." George Michael, and in particular his huge-selling 1987 album *Faith,* was another favourite of the teenage Bublé; he would later cover *Faith*'s 'Kissing A Fool', which became the lead single from his major-label debut album in 2003.

His admiration for George Michael's songcraft aside, there was no doubt in Bublé's mind about where his musical loyalties lay. "Growing up, I was listening to the stuff that young people listen to – Pearl Jam and Oasis and Dr Dre – but it never gave me the real spark that I got listening to Sinatra or Tony Bennett. Those guys are like the [Canadian ice hockey legend Wayne] Gretzkys of music. You just can't be average with this kind of material. You can't hide. You have to be able to *swing*."

He is at pains to stress that not only did his musical influences stretch to rock, but he also made efforts to fit in sartorially. "I had long hair, two earrings through each ear, snow-washed jeans, the high-top trainers. My denim jacket had 'I love Guns N' Roses' and 'I love AC/DC' written all over it." Photographs from the school's yearbook for his senior year bear out the fact that Michael did indeed have an earring in his left ear.

In an interview with the *Times Educational Supplement*, he spoke in detail about his time at Cariboo Hill. "I sometimes felt a little alone. I suppose I was an eccentric kid. I loved acting and music. I wasn't part of the hip crowd and I felt pressure to fit in. At times it was hard for me, but I enjoyed classes and I loved meeting girls. I also loved to sing and I'd often perform spontaneously in the cafeteria at lunchtime. I even delivered singing telegrams to raise money for the school. When I think about it now, how embarrassing does that sound? But it was sweet and fun to do."

Bublé was torn between the desire to conform and an equally strong impulse to be different. He later explained the conflict in a way that applied equally to his music as to his adolescence. "I think it's really hip to be nerdy, and I have a friend who always says 'cool is as cool does'." Known as Mike Bublé at Cariboo, he might not have been good enough at ice hockey but he made it onto the soccer team, although he was a long way from being, in North American parlance, a jock. "As a kid, I was really kind of naive and shy. I was the class clown, but I wasn't an aggressive kid. In sport, I didn't want to ruffle feathers I was quite shy – so shy, as a matter of fact, that I spent a lot of time pretending. I think that's why I am who I am today. I liked being by myself."

Academically, he was unremarkable. "I never felt that I was a smart guy – that I was an intelligent person. Socially, I was OK, but academically, I was always really self-conscious." He told the *TES* that he was "an average student – my attention span was pretty short. I didn't always feel challenged, and I would get bored easily.

"I enjoyed English and social studies, but I just couldn't understand maths. Having said that, my favourite teacher was my 10th grade maths teacher, Mr Clarke. He started every class with a puzzle based on linear thinking. I wasn't very good, but I would always try hard and I sensed he was aware of that. He appreciated the amount of effort I put in. And he didn't fail me; I guess he realised that wouldn't send the right message to myself or others who were struggling. I missed Mr Clarke when he got sick and didn't come back to school. I was crushed. He was the only one who made maths fun."

Michael Bublé graduated from high school in 1993. In his yearbook entry, he thanked God and his family and slipped in several song titles as well as coded references to friends: "My five years at Cariboo were unforgettable, to all the girls I've loved before and to the GRG Jr's and New Edition, may all of your dreams come true. I'd like to thank my parents and wish all the best of luck to Brandee and Crystal. A special thanks to God, who's given me all the friends and family that have made my life the greatest. And God bless Harry Connick Jr for learning the recipe for making love. RA, Grandma, Grandpa, CT. It had to be you!"

The Canadian school system is similar to that of the United States. Students graduate with a diploma in their final year, usually aged 18. The diplomas are awarded at a graduation ceremony. Characteristically, Michael took the opportunity to perform at his, claiming, "One of the reasons I started singing was so I could meet girls. I wasn't a dork at school, but I was just as insecure as any other boy."

But Michael must surely have wondered if the best way to achieve his goal would be to sing with a rock band. Answering British girl group The Saturdays many years later on his *An Audience With...* TV special, he admitted it was "the most honest and probably sad answer" he had given that evening. "Yes, in the hugest way possible. When I was about 12 or 13 years old, I thought that Eddie Vedder was the next coming of Elvis Presley. I was a kid, I loved Springsteen and Guns N' Roses and all that – but I also liked Sinatra and it wasn't that cool to like Sinatra, I guess. Or I was afraid it wasn't, so I'd sit there with my Walkman on and pretend to listen to the Beastie Boys or something!"

Two more important ingredients were added to the musical stew at the end of the Eighties. The more unlikely, perhaps was Vancouverite rocker Bryan Adams. Bublé recalled that his parents "brought me this record and I was infatuated by the fact that this man had had this huge success and that he was from my hometown. I dreamt of being a singer and an entertainer even from the time I was five or six years old, so to know that this guy had done it was really inspirational."

The namecheck for Harry Connick Jr (and his song 'Recipe For Love') in his yearbook entry was also significant. Connick's career has certain parallels with Bublé's own. Connick also learned his trade over many years of struggle, mainstream success arriving 12 years after his independent-label debut, when director Rob Reiner asked him to provide the soundtrack for 1989 movie *When Harry Met Sally*. Its double platinum sales and Grammy Award for Best Male Jazz Vocal Performance showed Michael that there was still a market for that style of music and that standards like 'It Had To Be You' and 'Let's Call The Whole Thing Off' could be reinterpreted to appeal to modern audiences.

Connick's success inspired Bublé to enter high-school talent shows. Looking back, Bublé pinpointed his importance. "He kind of made it cool, made it OK for me to come out of the closet and say I love this music, too." There was another crucial aspect, one familiar to any boy who ever wanted to join a band or sing on stage. "I remember all of a sudden seeing this guy's picture on girls' lockers…"

The tapes Grandpa Mitch compiled for him also came in handy when, for six years from the age of 14, Michael spent the long summer vacation on his father's boat, the *Dalmacia*, initially as an ordinary crew member. A commercial vessel, the 82-foot *Dalmacia* trawled for freshwater salmon swimming close to the surface using a large net, or seine, suspended from its side. The round trip to Alaska occupied the whole of the summer and Michael spent numerous hours absorbed in the music playing through the earphones of his Walkman.

"I was really into Tony Bennett," he said of one expedition. "I remember [my grandfather] making me mix tapes and me sitting on my father's fishing boat, listening to, you know, 'I Left My Heart In San Francisco' by Tony Bennett." His vocal chords were exercised regularly, too. "Every single day and I sang and really I didn't shut up. I remember sitting on the bow of the boat by the coiled ropes by the anchor, just singing away."

The *Dalmacia* was docked in Port Edward, a tiny, historic fishing village, site of the oldest surviving salmon cannery in Canada and some 800 kilometres from Burnaby. On arriving at Port Edward, Lewis recalled, his son and the other crewmen would head for nearby Prince Rupert, the main city on British Columbia's north coast, a bustling port at the very edge of Canada's northern wilderness. "[They] would jump on a bus and go into Prince Rupert to have a few cold drinks. But, of course, they never told me anything until we left port – so later I heard Michael went to the Surf Club for karaoke night. There he was singing Elvis songs to a very tough-looking crowd. The rest of the crew was fearful for their lives. It turns out Michael was a real hit and the crowd ended up buying him drinks." Moreover, Michael's musical horizons were expanded further by swapping tapes with like-minded students he encountered in Prince Rupert, jazz devotees who were also working their vacation.

Such diversions aside, the teenager was not enamoured of the life of a Pacific fisherman, describing it as, "The most deadly physical work I'll ever know in my lifetime. We'd be gone for two, sometimes three months at a time and the experience of living and working among guys over twice my age taught me a lot about responsibility and what it means to be a man." The hours were long – an 18-hour day was standard – and the conditions awful, torrential rain and sub-zero temperatures. "I'd be sitting there, freezing cold, tired, just *dying*. I'd cry and say to my dad, 'You asshole, how could you make your son come out here?' I was terrified I'd have to work like he did." Lewis Bublé has since traded the *Dalmacia* for a smaller boat, but he and Amber still go out fishing every summer.

Working on the boat also provided a lesson in interpersonal relations for the teenager. By the time he was 16, Michael had worked his way up the hierarchy to a position akin to first mate. When he attempted to belittle an older and larger crewmate, he came off second best in the subsequent confrontation via a headbutt. "It taught me common respect. And I never, *ever* talk down to people."

And a fisherman's life was hard work. Up at four in the morning, in bed at 11, it was a lifestyle Michael could only follow for a while. But he remembers it well enough to have a lifelong aversion to salmon. He also went to bed with Vaseline on his hands to make sure that his rope burns wouldn't crack open.

Michael quickly realised that he was not cut out for the demanding physical work, and singing came to represent his most likely escape route. The summer fishing trips became a kind of aversion therapy. "It was so hard and nasty and a lot of the times I'd be terrified that this is what I'd have to do for my life. My father would come up to me and say, 'Michael, don't use your hands, please use your head. You don't want to have to work like I do.'"

When he became an international star, Bublé discussed the contrast in lifestyles. "I can remember sitting on the bow of my dad's fishing boat, I would be dreaming of this. Sometimes I wake up and ask myself, 'Will I wake up this morning and be back on the boat?'" The lessons learned stayed with him. "I don't take for granted the position I'm in now." The experience helped keep him grounded when success finally arrived. "I know what it's like to have a tough job, so it makes me really appreciate the fact that all I have to do now is get up on stage and sing with great musicians."

He shares the grounding a pre-stardom working life gave him with the late, great country legend Johnny Cash, who said: "For thirty-one years I've been staying in the finest hotels and travelling first class. But my roots are in the working man. I remember very well how it is to pick cotton ten hours a day, or to plough, or how to cut wood. I remember it so well, I guess, because I don't intend to ever try to do it again."

Back on dry land, Grandpa Mitch paid for Michael to take singing lessons. His tutor was Joseph Shore, a highly respected baritone renowned for his performances in Verdi's operas. At the time, Shore was teaching at the Music Instruction Faculty of the University of British Columbia in Vancouver.

As has now passed into Bublé folklore, Mitch offered free plumbing work for any local club owners who would employ the underage singer. In 2005, Michael related the origins of the practice. "At 15, when I told my family singing was what I wanted to do, he took me to a hotel in Vancouver where there was a corporate event. There was a little band up on stage, and he asked the band if I could go up on stage and the singer said, 'Absolutely *not*!' My grandpa said, 'Okay, listen, you let my grandkid up there, I'll put in a free toilet for you.' When he figured out that it worked, he took me everywhere – nightclubs, singing lessons, jazz clubs. He used to take me to talent contests. He did everything for me; he loved me. He loved good music, good songs. To this day, I would say that he gets more out of it than I do."

Even Mitch did not foresee the heights to which Michael's career would eventually ascend. "I said to my grandpa, 'So, grandpa, did you ever think it would be like this?' And he says, 'No, I thought you'd be the opening act for somebody in Las Vegas.' And I kind of just looked at him and went, like, 'Thanks a lot, grandpa.'" Family banter aside, Michael has also said that "grandpa always thought I had it, even when I really didn't."

In his 2008 book about highly successful people, *Outliers*, Malcolm Gladwell theorises that most people who are remarkably successful in their chosen field become so after putting in an average of 10,000 hours' practice, citing as examples The Beatles and Bill Gates. Michael Bublé put in the hours, listening, learning and practising even before his long apprenticeship in Vancouver, Toronto and Los Angeles. "I can't tell you how many hours I studied Frank Sinatra or listened to Mel Tormé and visualised myself singing and performing like they did. I even had thoughts like, 'What would I say?', 'How would I move?' or 'What jokes would I tell?'"

As Grandpa Mitch had realised, Bublé was a natural performer, whether it be on stage in tiny clubs, in the school canteen, at shopping malls, as a singing telegram on St Valentine's Day or as a wedding singer. Of the experience as a singing telegram, he reminisced, tongue in cheek, that, "Ten out of 11 times they wouldn't [tip]. They'd say, 'I want you to sing it louder.' And I'd be, 'But it's a *ballad*.'"

With regard to performance, he recalled, "I knew that I wanted to do this from an early age. I was always pretty comfortable onstage. I'm actually more comfortable onstage in front of 10,000 people than talking one-on-one with someone. I have a lot more social anxiety in smaller situations." Live performance has never held any fears, and he has absolutely no pre-show rituals or superstitions. "I pee... and that's about it!" he laughs.

His stagecraft was quick to develop. "I played really tough, raunchy places. When I started singing at 16, I was playing seedy nightclubs and strip clubs, and I was just a little kid. I was far too comfortable for my own good. I just enjoyed every second – I soaked it up. And some nights, if I really put my mind to it, I could make it wild, to the point where there were girls naked and there were people having sex. It was just *wild*. I could make it a party. And these clubs used to hire me because, on a Monday night, they'd be lined up down the street because I was raunchy and had so much fun."

Early Life

Interviewed in 2009 on Australian television, he revealed how he dealt with playing in front of audiences in strip clubs who were most definitely not there to listen to him, "With humour. I think the simple answer [is] – with humour. Just as simple as I'd be in a strip bar and I'd come onto the microphone and I would say, 'OK, guys, look at how excited you are to see me! You don't want the girls to come by, you want *me*!'"

At 18, Michael's life was at a crossroads. He had left school and was still working on Lewis's boat during the summer to earn money while gigging wherever and whenever he could. "I worked every bar, club, cruise ship and shopping mall."

He needed his remarkable powers of perseverance to stick at it. Amber recalled that her son always displayed a "ridiculous faith that it would happen, nothing would stop him". Grandpa Mitch's belief in Michael's talent was unwavering, but his was now a lone voice. "All the people, including the people who love me, said that it's not going to happen. They said never expect that to happen for you, because it won't. Because the kind you music you make it'll have limited appeal, limited radio and all that."

His persistence paid off when he won two local talent contests, the second of which introduced him to the first person in the entertainment industry to detect something special in the teenager. A local entrepreneur with a reputation for straight talking, Beverly Delich set up Silver Lining Management in 1989. Part of her mission was to seek out new talent in the Greater Vancouver area, which involved organising talent contests. One such took place at Big Bamboo, a Vancouver nightspot, and Michael entered, singing the jazz standard 'All Of Me'. Afterwards Delich told him he had won and asked his age. Honest as ever and suspecting that the game was up, Bublé confessed that he was 18, leaving Delich with no option but to disqualify him because Canadian law stipulates 19 as the minimum age for entry to nightclubs.

Like all good storytellers, Bublé later exaggerated the incident for comic effect, claiming that he was 16 and that he "drew on a moustache and sideburns, snuck in and won the contest. The next day I spoke to Beverly Delich who ran the place, she told me I was underage and had been disqualified."

The fair at the Pacific National Exhibition (PNE) is held annually in Hastings Park, Vancouver during late August and early September. The 17-day event is one of the largest fairs in North America; a late-summer jamboree popular with children and adults alike, it celebrated its 100th anniversary in 2010. There are pig races, dog shows and exhibitions by Shaolin monks along with the usual fairground rides. Forming a vital part of the event are three talents contests, kids (6–12), youth (13–21) and extra years of zest (over 55s).

As well as booking the entertainment for the fair, Beverly Delich was responsible for organising and running the competitions. These were serious affairs lasting the duration of the fair, and Delich invited respected figures in the local entertainment industry to be judges. The contests were well-liked by fairgoers and oversubscribed in terms of would-be contestants. Entrants were drawn from all corners of the musical spectrum including pop, rock, country, classical and jazz. Beverly Delich's horizons were not limited to any particular genre.

The youth section was the major prize and the most hotly contested, and Delich arranged for Bublé to enter the 1995 contest. For him, it was an opportunity not only to perform for a large crowd but also to sing with the big band led by legendary Vancouverite Dal Richards. Canada's king of swing, Richards had worked with Frank Sinatra, Bing Crosby, Sammy Davis Jr and Dean Martin when they were in town and had made his name in the Forties when Vancouver's night life was said to equal San Francisco's. A stalwart of the PNE, he directed the Dal Richards Orchestra at the event for over 70 years.

Bublé remembered the contest clearly, for several reasons. "My grandfather had always hoped that some day I'd get to meet Dal – my grandfather! Then I entered the PNE Youth Talent Search and there he was, larger than life. It was such a neat feeling to be this young kid and get up there with this great big band and get to sing for those big audiences – mixed, not just older people, a lot of kids, which proved to me that this music I was singing was palatable to everyone."

Beverly's faith in his ability was justified when he emerged victorious in the vocal performance category. As part of his reward, he went to Memphis with Beverly in the autumn to take part in the International Talent Search, including a tour of the state of Tennessee where Elvis grew up. His win at the PNE also entitled him enter in the 1996 Canadian Youth Talent Competition. This prestigious national contest is held in each of Canada's ten provinces and three territories on a rotating basis. In February 1996, Michael travelled with Beverly to compete but was not placed in one of the three prize-winning categories.

The relationship between singer and Svengali, however, was soon to take on a new phase. "I was in an airplane with her coming back from a talent contest that she had taken me to, and I asked her to be my manager on the plane. I said I will give you 15 per cent. So, Beverly looks at me and asks, 'Do you know how much 15 per cent of nothing is?'" Despite pointedly asking Michael, "Why do you think you need a manager?" Delich agreed to fulfil the role and quickly started to make things happen for the youngster.

The first step on any journey is the most important, and Michael had started his one-man musical mission. If he had known how far he still had to go, it would surely have seriously daunted his optimistic spirit. But as he entered his twenties and contemplated his future, the singing fisherman certainly had reason to smile.

CHAPTER 2

The Struggling Years

One of the first fruits of the Delich-Bublé partnership was Michael's recording debut, *First Dance*. Made with Beverly Delich's guidance and encouragement, the 1996 mini-album contained just six tracks: 'Learnin' The Blues', 'I've Got You Under My Skin', 'Just One More Dance', 'All Of Me', 'One Step At A Time' and 'I'll Be Seeing You'.

First Dance is the only recording Bublé would make of four of these songs. Of the other two, 'All Of Me', the first song Michael ever sang on stage, was finally re-recorded for 2010's *Crazy Love*. The other long-time staple of the Bublé repertoire, 'I've Got You Under My Skin', was reworked in 2005 for *It's Time*.

'Learnin' The Blues' was a Fifties song that Frank Sinatra took to number two in the US charts, and it had later been recorded as a duet by Ella Fitzgerald and Louis Armstrong. In recent years, it has also attracted the attention of British-Georgian chanteuse Katie Melua. 'Just One More Dance' was less well known.

'One Step At A Time' was performed to a sparse acoustic-guitar-and-finger-snap backing, while 'I'll Be Seeing You', penned by

Irving Kahal and Sammy Fain in 1938 and a World War II favourite with servicemen and their sweethearts, went totally the other way. Its weighty horn and violin arrangement was suitably redolent of the Forties.

Recorded in eight days, *First Dance* was part showcase for Michael's voice, part calling card and part gift for friends and family, especially Grandpa Mitch. The money for the recording, £6,000, came from his grandfather. Four years later, the cost of the recording would prove a sound investment when the CD would play a vital part in his breakthrough.

First Dance was never intended for wider public circulation. In December 2003, shortly after the success of his first album proper, Bublé told BBC Radio 2's Michael Parkinson, an early champion of his work, that *First Dance*, together with its independently released successors *BaBalu* (2001) and *Dream* (2002), had been removed from the market because he felt that they were not of sufficiently high quality. Barring a change of heart, all three albums will remain collector's items, highly prized by Bublé completists.

The same year, 1996, also saw Michael make a tentative start to his acting career, with two small 'blink-and-you-miss-it' roles as an extra. Michael had been interested in acting since high school and many of his musical heroes – Frank Sinatra, Bing Crosby and Dean Martin among them – had appeared in movies with varying degrees of success; naturally, he jumped at any chance to follow in their footsteps. Vancouver is a major centre for film and television production, often doubling as a location for other North American cities, with the added advantage of spectacular natural features close by. Together with Beverly Delich's local showbusiness connections, this gave Bublé the chance to gain some experience in front of the cameras.

His first appearance was in a TV movie, *Death Game*, retitled *Mortal Challenge* for video and DVD release. Produced by prolific cult film-maker Roger Corman, known with good reason as king of the B movies, the film concerned the aftermath of a devastating earthquake that had divided Los Angeles into two communities – rich and poor. A young-looking Michael, listed in the credits as 'Mike Bublé', can be seen for a few seconds in the background as one of 12 'Drome Groupies', but his presence is largely overshadowed by voluptuous villainess Felicia, played by Korrine St Onge. The movie is now largely forgotten, Michael's cameo the only thing saving it from total obscurity.

Filmed in Vancouver for its first five seasons, *The X-Files* was the defining cult television show of the Nineties. Masterminded by Chris Carter, it followed two FBI special agents as they investigated unsolved cases of paranormal phenomena, and its story arcs concerned alien abduction and conspiracy theories. Michael featured as one of three anonymous submarine sailors seen in a black-and-white flashback to events in World War II. He enjoyed a little more screen time than his previous role, including a fleeting close-up, while his acting consisted of pulling expressions of horror and surprise at the strange events in the sub. His contribution spans two episodes from *The X-Files*' third season, produced in 1996, 'Piper Maru' and the conclusion of the storyline in 'Apocrypha'. He did not receive an on-screen credit for his contribution, however.

Under Beverly Delich's guidance, Bublé continued to work as hard as always, never declining a gig, not even one that required him to don the red-and-white costume and false beard of a singing Santa Claus, for which he received the sum of $80. Much more up his street were dates at various Vancouver venues, the Purple Onion (a cabaret club), the Cecil Hotel, the Vogue Theatre and the Commodore Ballroom among them.

"I worked every bar, club, cruise ship and shopping mall," recalls Bublé. Playing bars, in particular, was a trial, especially when he felt not enough attention was being paid. He once recalled playing to a handful of people who refused to stop their conversation and listen. "They'd be like, 'Fucking shut up, we're trying to talk here.' They didn't realise getting hit by a microphone really hurt…"

Some audiences could be even less friendly. He told Michael Parkinson in 2007 that he experienced "people throwing cigarettes at me, you know, 'Do [Lynyrd Skynyrd rock anthem] "Freebird"', stuff like that." Persistent as ever, he achieved his first residency at the Georgia Street Bar and Grill on West Georgia Street, and from there moved a step up to what would become a twice-weekly spot at the BaBalu Lounge.

The Cuban-themed BaBalu was situated on the ground floor of the Nelson-at-Granville Comfort Inn at 654 Nelson Street in the Yaletown district of downtown Vancouver. It was named after a song written by Margarita Lecuona and made famous by Cuban singer Miguelito Valdés and big-band leader Desi Arnaz, a man better known for his appearances with his wife Lucille Ball on television. However, the BaBalu is unlikely to see a plaque commemorating its position as a step on the Bublé stairway to stardom. The venue was gutted by fire in 2001 and an Irish theme pub, Doolins, now stands on the site.

The stage at the BaBalu was tiny with a backdrop of red curtains. Musical accompaniment was provided by a house band, The Smokin' Section. Michael faced the nightly challenge of going eyeball to eyeball with the paying customers, who were more likely to be interested in the bar's extensive range of cocktails than listening to a singer. Nevertheless, playing to patrons who were, at best, indifferent was not necessarily a disadvantage, as he explained. "They came to meet a woman or get wasted, but I learned my craft. It taught me how not to reek of desperation, how to step back and try to be charismatic and let them fall in love with me."

Local radio announcer and friend Buzz Bishop, whose station sponsored nights at the BaBalu, recalled the young man's commitment to giving everything. "Michael would put all his energy and passion into it. He treated every show as if he were headlining in Vegas." He thrived in the club's intimate atmosphere and began to attract fans of his own.

By the end of 1997, Michael had established himself as a name attraction; flyers outside the club announced 'Michael Bublé – Sundays and Mondays – Cool Room, Swingin' Sounds, Stylin' People.' Another DJ, lounge music specialist Jason Manning of CKST Vancouver, frequently acted as master of ceremonies. Bublé's association with the club would last for two years and the lessons he learned would stay with him forever.

A short drive north from the BaBalu along Highway 99 is Granville Island (Granville was the original name for Vancouver). Formed from landfill around two sandbars in Vancouver's False Creek, the island was once a centre of heavy industry. Now devoted to leisure activities, it is home to two of the three stages operated by the Arts Club Theatre Company, the Granville Island Stage and the Revue Stage. The name Arts Club is slightly misleading; the company is a major player, the largest organisation of its kind in western Canada, with an impressive reputation for pioneering new Canadian drama.

In 1996, writer and director Dean Regan was putting together a musical revue called *Red Rock Diner*. A native of Vancouver, Regan had already written and directed *A Closer Walk With Patsy Cline* for the Arts Club and subsequently toured the United States with it. *Red Rock Diner* was more than just another jukebox musical; like the Patsy Cline show, it aimed for an authentic recreation of its musical genre.

The show was both an homage to early rock 'n' roll and a tribute to legendary British Columbian disc jockey Red Robinson. The first man in Canada to play 'race' records by black artists, Robinson was a pivotal figure in introducing rock 'n' roll music to Canada in general and to Vancouver in particular. He had hung out with Elvis Presley and introduced The Beatles on stage in Vancouver in 1964. *Red Rock Diner* was a vision of Americana from a Canadian perspective.

The Arts Club Theatre Company's highly respected artistic managing director, Bill Millerd, was involved in the production and the casting. He heard from Beverly Delich of a young singer who was capable of filling the role of an Elvis lookalike. As Michael recalls, Millerd took some convincing. "I can remember singing at the Georgia Bar and Grill, and when they hired me for BaBalu, I was *so* excited. Bill Millerd of the Arts Club Theatre was invited to come down and see my act, and he was just starting the musical *Red Rock Diner*. I urged him to let me perform in the musical. He really felt I wasn't right for the show. He did come down, not once but four times, because he wasn't sure. I'm glad I was able to change his mind."

Millerd's caution was understandable; Bublé had no theatrical experience and was not primarily a rock 'n' roll vocalist. The show required him to dance as well as sing. In his favour, he was an accomplished mimic, able to imitate both Presley's singing style and speaking voice, and, as the cover of the privately pressed *First Dance* shows, he resembled the young, bequiffed Elvis. Musical theatre was a new departure for Michael: submerging his identity into an ensemble was something very different to his ambitions as a solo performer. Nevertheless, he was keen to be a part of such a prestigious production.

Standing out from the rest of the cast was a striking, long-legged brunette called Debbie Timuss, a regular actress/dancer at Arts Club productions. She was younger than Michael but more experienced in musical theatre. A former cheerleader for the short-lived Vancouver Grizzlies basketball team, Debbie helped him with his dancing and taught him the choreography for *Red Rock Diner*. It marked the start of a relationship that would last for eight years, although Michael and Debbie would not become an item until two years later.

Set in the diner of the title during the first act, and in a high-school gym for the second, the fast-moving two-hour revue packed in more than 20 songs. It demanded high levels of energy and stamina from the performers, with a daily schedule of evening and matinée shows. In the first half, Michael played the young Elvis singing 'Blue Suede Shoes' with backing from a crack five-piece rock 'n' roll band specially assembled for the production. Other individual spots came in the shape of Marilyn Monroe and Johnnie Ray tributes.

Debbie Timuss was singled out by one reviewer for "perhaps the best solo performance of the night" which was "remarkably funny and acrobatic". The same review praised Michael along with his colleagues as "extremely talented in their roles". Act Two saw him morph into the chubby Seventies Elvis, and the show concluded with an ensemble rendition of Roy Orbison's epic ballad 'Crying'.

The show ran for the summer of 1997 at Granville Island to such an enthusiastic audience response that its residency was extended until the end of September. After that, the production went on the road in Canada and the United States. Michael looked back fondly on the experience. "It was without a doubt one of the best times I have ever had in my career. Being part of that ensemble changed all of our lives." Despite the positives gained from the show, rock 'n' roll was not the musical avenue he wished to pursue. Elvis impersonators were legion in the United States and Michael Bublé was determined to be his own man, not a tribute act, although he was always quick to acknowledge the influences of the masters, including Presley. "I stole everything I could from these great singers," he admitted.

The year of 1997 saw Michael make his first inroads into television, this time as a singer rather than an extra in drama shows. His first national exposure in Canada was in *Big Band Boom!*, a documentary about the swing era in the Thirties and Forties broadcast on the country's cable arts channel, Bravo. Michael made an appearance as a crooner. Director Mark Glover Masterson garnered a 1998 Silver Screen Award at the US International Film and Video Festival in Chicago for his creation. He also received a nomination at the 1998 Hot Docs! Festival in Toronto.

Beverly Delich's hard work then secured Michael what amounted to his biggest break yet, regular appearances on *Gabereau Live*, an afternoon chat/variety show networked nationally on CTV. The eponymous host, Vicki Gabereau, was making the transition to television after 12 years on CBC radio. Beginning in September 1997, the daily programme was made in Vancouver and aired live during its first season. Local boy Bublé was in an ideal position to answer producer David Fuller's call to fill in when other guests pulled out at the eleventh hour. It was here that Michael first met and impressed fellow British Columbian Diana Krall, the future Mrs Elvis Costello, who had already made a name for herself as a jazz singer. They would remain firm friends thereafter, often trying to boost each other's profile by mentions in interviews.

In addition to singing, Michael took part in interviews with garrulous host Gabereau, known variously as 'the chat queen', 'the princess of gab' and, less favourably, 'the grand-dame of foot-in-mouth'. Here he began to learn another important part of his trade – a successful interview is a performance in itself, and by using his natural charm in that environment he could win many friends. Never one to forget his roots, he would make a sentimental return for the final *Vicki Gabereau Show* in 2005 as a gesture of gratitude.

Another television appearance followed in October, when Michael was featured on British Columbia Television News' *Eye On The Street* feature. With his hair teased into a *Red Rock Diner* quiff, he again bore a noticeable resemblance to the young Elvis Presley. The interview took place while he was back in Vancouver before travelling to Missouri with the show. To the accompaniment of piano, Michael gave a performance for the camera alone and the clip provides a tantalising glimpse of the BaBalu Lounge.

Interviewer Zack Spencer made play of the similarity between the names 'Bublé' and 'BaBalu', while Michael stated his intention to record a live album at the venue. Although this never appeared, the seed was sown and he would name his 2001 album after the club. There is also an early mention of grandfather Mitch Santagà's influence in introducing him to jazz and swing on crackly old vinyl records. Michael insisted, as he would many times in the future, that he also listened to contemporary music like Guns N' Roses and hip-hop while growing up. His family continued to accept his career path, and their encouragement was as vital now as it had ever been. "They were incredibly supportive," he recalled in 2010, "and I know for a fact that I wouldn't be here if it wasn't for them. From the start they said go for it."

Interestingly, the *BaBalu* album contained Michael's interpretations of several Mills Brothers songs, including 'Lazy River', in homage to his grandfather. He also cut his grandfather's all-time favourite, 'You'll Never Know', along with standards like 'Can't Help Falling In Love', 'Mack The Knife' and, somewhat bizarrely, the 'Spider-Man Theme'.

As well as TV interviewer Zack Spencer, support in the Vancouver media also came from legendary British Columbia disc jockey Jack Cullen. A big-band enthusiast and part-time crooner himself, Cullen urged Michael to vary the pace of his set by singing more ballads in between the up-tempo numbers, advice the singer was happy to heed.

Bublé's performances as an ersatz Elvis in *Red Rock Diner* had been sufficiently impressive to land him a part in Dean Regan's next jukebox musical, *Forever Swing*. Initially known simply as *Swing*, it enjoyed the distinction of being the opening production at the Stanley Industrial Alliance Stage in downtown Vancouver, the Arts Club's third venue and 650-seat flagship theatre. Beginning with a hugely successful residency in October 1998, the show's original four-week run was extended to 11 because of unprecedented demand for tickets.

Subtitled *The Big Band Musical Revue, Forever Swing* was a similarly dynamic exercise to *Red Rock Diner*. The nostalgic focus shifted back in time to the Forties and featured 27 songs, among them 'It Don't Mean A Thing If It Ain't Got That Swing', 'The Sheik Of Araby' and 'Sing, Sing, Sing'. Michael's big number was 'Begin The Beguine'. He was again part of an ensemble cast consisting of 11 singer/dancers, plus a 13-piece band that gained universal praise; Bublé was in his element singing in front of them. Along with the band, it was the other veteran of *Red Rock Diner,* Debbie Timuss, who caught the eye of the *Washington Post* critic, drawing generous praise for her dancing skills.

Michael was singled out by online reviewer Denis Armstrong of jam.canoe.ca. Discussing a performance in Ottawa, he said, "But if the show were to boast one single feature that puts this production head-and-shoulders above most touring musicals, it would be singer Michael Bublé. A dead ringer for young Frank Sinatra, Bublé is not some bobby-soxer wannabe but an outstanding singer in the mould of the Rat Pack, who could carry the show off himself. Fortunately, he gets lots of competition from the talented musicians and dancers with whom he shares the bus."

The first half followed the fictional Tommy Vickers Band on tour in America just before the Second World War. The second was set in a recreation of the London Palladium of the Forties during the victory celebrations. The emphasis on dance was strong, with tap routines, ballroom dancing, Lindy hop and jitterbug. Regan even found space for gimmicks like a fire-eating bikini-clad woman. Nevertheless, the music was treated with respect and recreated authentically. A soundtrack album featuring 15 songs by the cast, including Bublé's rendition of 'Begin The Beguine', was only on sale at the shows and is today another hard-to-find collector's item.

Forever Swing kept Michael busy for much of 1999. Demand for tickets was so high that it was brought back to the Stanley Theatre for the summer season. Then it went on tour in Canada, finishing at Toronto's historic Elgin and Winter Gardens Theatres, the only remaining stacked Edwardian theatres in the world; *Forever Swing* played in the lower level, the Elgin. Critical and popular acclaim saw an extension of its original six-week residency until the end of December 1999.

Michael and Debbie's slowly developing love affair had blossomed during the production of *Forever Swing*. Now very much a couple, they elected to remain in Toronto full-time, hoping that living in a bigger city would introduce him to a wider audience and improve his chances of finding the elusive break which would kick-start his career.

Michael took gigs wherever he could, one of which was singing with a jazz trio at the Reservoir Lounge, a downtown nightspot that specialised in swing. His association with the venue would last right up to the promotion for his debut major-label album in 2003. Meanwhile, Debbie was finding plentiful work as a dancer-actress. But as he approached his 25th birthday in September 2000, Michael was starting to fear that, despite all the adventures and experiences of the previous nine years, he would never break out of the small-club scene.

Back in Vancouver, the ever-industrious Beverly Delich was still hustling on behalf of her client. Towards the end of 1999, he appeared in a promotional video for Air Canada that focused on the natural beauty of the British Columbian landscape, said to have inspired many artists. Introduced as a 'young and talented crooner', Bublé reveals that he wrote a song, 'Dumb Ol' Heart', when he was just 14 on his father's fishing boat in Campbell River, a city on the east coast of Vancouver Island known as the 'Salmon Capital of the World'. "I wrote it out of loneliness," Michael explained, "probably for a girl that I hadn't met yet." There was a clip of him singing the song using an old-fashioned radio microphone, looking every inch the crooner he was claimed to be.

Shortly afterwards, 'Dumb Ol' Heart' featured in a Canadian film, *Here's To Life,* playing over the closing credits. Released in January 2000, the road movie starred Eric McCormack, famous at the time for his starring role in the sitcom *Will And Grace.* Despite favourable critical notices, *Here's To Life* performed poorly at the box office – so poorly, in fact, that a soundtrack album never saw the light of day. This remains a source of frustration to Bublé fans as the movie contains a second self-penned number 'I've Never Been In Love Before', in addition to a performance of 'When You're Smiling', the much-covered song made famous by Louis Armstrong.

The Genie Awards are the Canadian equivalent of the Oscars. *Here's To Life* won three and was nominated for another 11. Both of Michael's originals were up for the award for Best Achievement in Music – Original Song but neither managed to win. All three of his contributions can, however, be heard on the DVD.

Recognition from the film industry was welcome, but it wasn't enough to propel him into the major league. For the first time Michael's determination started to weaken. He seriously considered returning to Vancouver to study at the British Columbia Institute of Technology for a diploma in broadcast journalism. "I was about to give up, not because I felt sorry for myself, but because at some point I wanted to be a husband and a father. I knew that if I continued on, the harder it would be to get back into 'real life'. It's not that I wasn't talented, I just didn't get that break… If I was serious about wanting to have a life and make money, I knew that I would have to probably go back to school. I was thinking of going into the media, maybe as a television reporter or something like that. I enjoy my relationship with the camera. I have no problem being in front of the cameras."

A brief role in another road-trip movie was Michael's next showing in front of the camera, but it did little to alleviate his concerns. *Duets* was a comedy about the weird world of karaoke, starring Gwyneth Paltrow as part of an ensemble cast, which also included Eighties chart-topping singer Huey Lewis and Angie (*Police Woman*) Dickinson. Much of it was filmed in British Columbia; one location was Burnaby. Michael's time on screen was limited to a cameo crooning Frank Sinatra's 'Strangers In The Night'. It did not make the soundtrack album, which instead showcased material sung by Huey Lewis and marked Paltrow's debut as a singer. However, Bublé was at least listed in the film's credits as one of several 'Finale Singers'.

The movie premiered in September 2000, by which time Michael was ready to admit that his career had reached a dead end. "I had run out of money and run out of options, and the light at the end of the tunnel had just gone away. I busted my ass for nine years and, at some point, you think to yourself, 'I tried hard, potential is a lovely thing, but you can't feed your family on it.'"

But Beverly Delich refused to give in. "I called her almost in tears and said, 'Bevy, we tried so hard for so long, both of us,' and she said, 'Sweetheart, give me one more year. I promise you, one more year. This will be your year.'"

Michael elaborated on the fears that plagued him at this time. "I was so scared that I had spent so much time trying to make it that I had come too far. It was either I need to do I don't know what, or quit. I was 26 years old and I had no money, and I wanted to have kids one day. If I went back to school then, by the time I got out of school, I'd have been 31. Then by the time I paid off my debts, I'd have been 34. All of a sudden, you start panicking."

The balance sheet was already sinking into the red. "The crummy thing was I was making such poor money and I was starting to go into debt. My musicians were getting more than I was." Cash-strapped

The Struggling Years

Michael was reluctantly drawn into the corporate world, playing events hosted by big companies to promote new products or simply as private parties. Sometimes regarded by musicians as selling out, such gigs are temptingly lucrative. Bublé would later bracket corporates, along with strip-joint gigs, as "horrible".

The artists booked are expected to provide familiar and appropriate music, usually as background entertainment to dining and drinking. Michael was unfazed by the prospect – after all, he had years of experience in winning over audiences who weren't there to listen to him. However, a performance at one particular firm's party was to prove the long-awaited turning point in his career, setting in motion a chain of events that would put an end to the years of struggle.

Every would-be star, no matter how talented and hard-working, can use a break. Being in the right place at the right time can shave months, years even, off the climb up stardom's staircase – and there's no doubting when and where it happened for Michael Bublé.

Michael's version of the story saw him drinking in the last-chance saloon. "I had moved to Toronto with my girlfriend, trying to make it, figuring it's a bigger city. I started doing the nightclubs, and I just wasn't making anything. My girlfriend was doing musical theatre and she was bringing home the bacon and paying for rent and all that other stuff. At some point, a big tour gig ended and we had no money. I couldn't afford to go home. So I took a corporate, a really kind of shoddy corporate gig for a couple, whatever it was, three thousand bucks or something, and it was enough to get me home."

Bublé's determination to play every gig as if he were headlining Las Vegas was about to reap dividends. In attendance was Michael McSweeney, a former Ottawa councillor, speechwriter to and confidant of ex-prime minister of Canada Brian Mulroney. Jazz fan McSweeney was impressed by Michael's performance, considering it something better than the usual fare on offer at such events. Afterwards McSweeney approached Michael to congratulate him – and what happened next is now firmly established in Bublé legend.

Blissfully unaware of McSweeney's status and connections, he regarded the older man as simply "a guy who liked my voice". Later Michael elaborated further: "He was really sweet, and I handed him the CD and kind of said, 'If you like it, take it home and listen to it with your wife and kids. If you don't, it'll make a great coaster for your desk.' The next day he called me and said, 'I'm the right-hand man to the Honourable Brian Mulroney and he's a fan.'"

Bublé had given McSweeney his very last copy of *First Dance*. McSweeney immediately played the CD for Mulroney and his Serbian-born wife Mila, and both were impressed with Michael's voice. Mila Mulroney invited the singer to Montreal to dine with the family and then to a party at their home in Palm Beach, Florida. "She just took me under her wing," the singer recalled. "She heard my story and we really clicked."

A connoisseur of the Great American Songbook, Brian Mulroney led the first Progressive Conservative administration in Canada for 26 years, becoming prime minister with a landslide majority in 1984. An ardent advocate of free trade, he presided for two terms, but his policies were increasingly controversial. In February 1993, towards the end of his second term and with his popularity at an all-time low, he resigned from politics, leaving the Canadian Tory party to be virtually wiped out at the General Election five months later.

Returning to his original profession as a lawyer, Mulroney went on to become an international business consultant, sitting on the board of many corporations where he made the acquaintance of some of the richest and most powerful people in the world. Bublé remarked that he and his family, like many ordinary Canadians, were not fans of Mulroney's politics and that he "wasn't necessarily the most popular prime minister we ever had." However, since his role in championing Michael's career, Bublé has revised his view somewhat, stating that his family and friends are now likely to view Mulroney as "the greatest prime minister ever". (The Mulroneys had also championed the cause of an up-and-coming French-Canadian singer, Celine Dion, several years earlier, and the exposure had led to her breaking out onto the international stage.)

The couple's daughter, Caroline, a law student at New York University, was shortly to be married to Andrew Lapham, a Princeton graduate and Internet businessman. His father, Lewis H Lapham, was an author and editor of the left-leaning, intellectual American *Harper's* magazine. The wedding was a spectacularly lavish affair, comprising a series of events with over 450 people attending. Guests included former American president George Bush and his wife Barbara, Queen Noor of Jordan, Prince Alexander of Yugoslavia and his Greek wife Katherine, former British premier Margaret Thatcher, US talk-show host Kathie Lee Gifford and Canadian media magnate Ted Rogers.

Preparations were already well advanced when Michael entered the orbit of McSweeney and, by association, the Mulroneys. It was Mila who came up with the idea that Michael should sing at the wedding, but with plenty of acts already booked there was some doubt as to whether room could be found. The indomitable Mila persuaded her husband that the young crooner should nevertheless be given his chance. Looking back, Michael put a typically humorous spin on the event. "I never sang at a wedding before either. I never wanted to be known as a wedding singer. I sang at one stupid wedding and now I'm the guy who sang at a wedding and got discovered." But this was no ordinary wedding and Michael Bublé was more than just a wedding singer.

The ceremony itself took place on Saturday September 16, 2000 in Westmount, Quebec. Crowds of well-wishers gathered outside the church, and the inevitable flock of paparazzi were drawn by the irresistibly newsworthy combination of high finance, politics, show business and royalty. Michael's performance would draw favourable press comment, but it was for different reasons that he would later describe the occasion as "the night my life changed".

The wedding, described as Montreal's social event of the year, had begun the previous night with a dinner hosted by the bridegroom's family. The service was preceded by a select luncheon for 50 people at the fabulously opulent Montreal offices of Paul Desmarais, a Canadian billionaire and friend of the Mulroneys. (The two lived in adjacent Palm Beach properties.) Afterwards there was a ball at the lush Le Windsor ballroom, and it was there that Michael performed. "He's been very good to me," he said of the bride's father, "and his family was wonderful and it was a real honour for me to do it – so, of course, I did it."

As dawn rose, around 100 people were still partying. On Sunday, the Mulroneys hosted brunch, at which the proud father took to the stage to sing 'Thank Heaven For Little Girls'. The secret service and the Royal Canadian Mounted Police watched over the entire proceedings. Everyone involved was required to sign a confidentiality agreement to protect the families' privacy.

The man Michael was set to impress was one David Foster. Not a name that would mean much to the average music fan, perhaps, but he was well-connected with a reputation in the business as a talent spotter *par excellence*. Nicknamed the Hit Man, he was a close friend of the Mulroneys.

Born in Victoria, the provincial capital of British Columbia, in 1949, Foster had enjoyed a career as keyboardist for one-hit wonders Skylark, whose 'Wallflower' made the US Top 10 in 1973. Although a follow-up proved elusive, Foster had arrived in Los Angeles and, on Skylark's break-up, set about establishing himself on the session scene as keyboardist, writer and producer. Such was his success that, in 1985, he was called upon to co-write and produce 'Tears Are Not Enough', Canada's contribution to African famine relief in the wake of Band Aid.

Foster was best known for his work with other artists, a roll call of big names having sought his services. But he also had a reputation for launching careers in spectacular fashion. All things considered, he was in an ideal position to add Michael to his stable of up-and-coming artists… if the young man could grab the opportunity with both hands.

Back at the wedding reception, the father of the bride ended up joining Michael on stage – along with Jackie Desmarais, socialite wife of Paul – for a three-way rendition of 'Paper Doll'. Explaining his enthusiasm for Michael, Mulroney later said that, "I'm what you call a frustrated saloon singer. I love music, and I love to sing – privately. When I heard him, the first thing I said to Mila was, 'This guy is a perfect cross between Frank Sinatra and Bobby Darin.' I was very high on him. And, of course, when I met him, he's such a polite, thoughtful and engaging young man."

After the wedding, the former prime minister took every opportunity to promote Michael's career. He told the chief executive of AOL Time Warner that Michael was one of the best singers he had ever heard and waxed lyrical to legendary American chat show host Merv Griffin about Buble's talents. Mulroney was even prepared break his self-imposed embargo on press interviews to promote Michael.

Although David Foster was at the wedding, he had come to socialise, not talent-spot. Understandably, therefore, he was initially resistant to Mulroney's overtures on behalf of his young protégé. "Brian told me, 'You're not going to believe this kid.' And I'm thinking, 'This is the last thing I want to do at a wedding, see some singer – a wedding singer.' But we were kind of transfixed." Foster later recalled that Buble "hit the stage like a lightning bolt". Michael's easy manner with the audience and its ecstatic reaction to him were not lost on Foster either. Among the other acts playing that night were Three's Company, a versatile seven-piece, well-versed in jazz, pop, disco and rock, but Bublé's star quality put him head and shoulders above the opposition.

For his part, Michael had been primed by the Mulroneys, who told him, "You know, our daughter's getting married and Foster's going to be there. You know, it would be a great chance for you to show off what you do and see if you can get some notice from him." Michael was keen to show what he could do. "Of course I jumped at the chance."

As Bublé recalls, Mulroney had his arm around his guest, "shaking him saying, 'Watch him, isn't he great? Just watch him.' So, he really kind of forced me upon David." Foster later confirmed this. "The prime minister was jumping up and down, saying, 'You're not going to believe this!' Of course, I hear that sort of thing all the time, and it's usually a disaster. But to Brian's credit, he spotted a good one. I was floored."

Fully aware that he had a unique opportunity to impress one of the industry's surest starmakers, Bublé had restructured his set accordingly. Although he performed the Kurt Weill-Bertolt Brecht standard 'Mack The Knife' – the signature tune for Bobby Darin, one of his idols, who had died two years before Bublé was born – Michael concentrated largely on self-penned material.

"Actually, at that time I was doing a lot of my originals. So that's what I sang. I got up on stage and did a bunch of my originals and Foster, I guess, was taken by it. He came up to me and he said, 'You're pretty good, kid. Do you want to come down to LA next week?' And I thought, 'Oh my God, I've *made* it.'"

In the event, Michael later confessed, things did not turn out to be quite as simple as that. "It took me a little while to get signed, and through that time the Mulroneys kept in contact with me a lot. Mila and Brian would call and say, 'I just put a call into David so we're putting the heat on him.' They were so supportive!"

But it was certainly true that Michael had achieved in a couple of hours what the previous years of struggle had not – a breakthrough into the mainstream music business. Where he went from now would be determined only by the limit of his talents.

CHAPTER 3

The First LP

Michael Bublé had certainly fallen on his feet when he secured that wedding gig back in September 2000 – for David Foster's credentials as a producer are impeccable. While he has been lauded, rightly, for his work with such international stars as Celine Dion, Barbra Streisand and Whitney Houston, working with the latter on the mega-platinum Dolly Parton cover 'I Will Always Love You' and *The Bodyguard* movie soundtrack, it is the sheer diversity of his work that has made him such an important figure within the music industry.

Where many of his peers have been happy to work within a specific musical genre, rarely venturing beyond the boundaries of one for fear of making mistakes in another, David has constantly pushed himself and his artists, who include Bryan Adams, Christina Aguilera, The Bee Gees, Andrea Bocelli, Mariah Carey, Chicago, Destiny's Child, Neil Diamond, Earth Wind & Fire, Gloria Estefan, Janet Jackson, Chaka Khan, Beyoncé Knowles, *NSYNC, Olivia Newton-John, Prince, Kenny Rogers, Boz Scaggs, Donna Summer and the aforementioned Dion, Streisand and Houston.

The First LP

The rewards for his musical endeavours have been immense. In 1995 he inked a deal with Warner Brothers giving him his own boutique label, 143 Records (the one, four, three being the respective numbers of letters in the phrase, 'I love you'). But David, perhaps wisely, decided to concentrate on what he knew best and gave day-to-day responsibility for running the label to his then manager, Brian Avnet, in order to concentrate on production.

One of the first acts he signed to 143 was glamorous singing siblings The Corrs, who recorded their debut album *Forgiven Not Forgotten* with him over a five-month spell. The album went on to become a major international success in Australia, Japan and Spain, and would eventually achieve platinum success in the UK, too, aided by a succession of reissued singles and television appearances that enabled The Corrs to become one of the most talked-about Irish bands in years.

After two years, David sold the 143 label back to Warner Brothers, reasoning that boutique labels were "in a bad spot". He retained his connection to the multinational giant, however, becoming a senior vice-president within the corporation and retaining the 143 name for a succession of releases. It seemed like a 'win-win' deal for all concerned.

One of the factors that has made Foster such a success is a total belief in what he does and in how he envisages each project. When he was asked to produce the Chicago album *Chicago 16*, he listened intently to the 13 songs the group wanted to record. When they had finished playing the thirteenth song, David called the group together and announced, "I've been a fan, but these songs suck. If I'm going to produce this album, we're going to have to write 13 new songs, because this isn't even close to what you should be doing."

The result was an album that hit the Top 10 in the US. The lead single, 'Hard To Say I'm Sorry', was written by David and lead singer Peter Cetera, with David explaining his preference for romantic songs thus. "I can't be Bruce Springsteen, much as I fantasise about being a rocker. I can only be who I am, and who I am is a guy who writes music that people make babies to – and I'm not going to apologise for it." When Cetera went solo, the pair continued to write songs together to chart-topping effect.

But David Foster is only human and has, by his own admission, made a few mistakes. One story he tells against himself is passing on the opportunity to produce the *Flashdance* soundtrack in 1984 as he could not see the project being a hit: "Welder by day, disco dancer by night? Are you kidding me?" That said, he has been proved right on more than enough occasions for his voice to carry more weight than even the hierarchy at Warner Brothers. American actor turned operatic tenor Josh Groban is a case in point.

At the time Josh signed with 143 Records, there were many within Warners who felt he would be a difficult artist to promote, with radio in particular likely to prove problematic. David Foster wasn't having any of it. "They were afraid they wouldn't be able to get a voice like that on radio. I love his natural ability in the pop and rock arena, but I love his sense of classics even more. He's a true musical force to be reckoned with." Groban, who has been compared with Bublé but is some six years his junior, went on to sell some 25 million records around the world.

While everything David Foster touches continues to turn to gold and platinum, he has one advantage when it comes to backing a hunch. Instead of convening endless meetings and talking shop, his is the *only* opinion that matters when it comes to signing artists to 143 Records and the direction they will take once there.

And yet, even David had his doubts about Michael Bublé! It was not his singing ability but the fact that, as he admitted, "I didn't know how to market this kind of music." Michael and his agent moved to Los Angeles to continue negotiating with Foster, and they settled on something of a compromise; David would produce an album if Michael could raise $500,000 to cover the production costs, something he eventually did through live performances, film work and the release of his last independent album, *Dreams*.

By the time they were ready to record together, however, David had had something of a change of heart, covering the whole $2 million cost of album production under his 143 Records agreement, even though there were no formal assurances of support from Warner Brothers.

Indeed, Foster went even further. As well as agreeing to record his protégé, David Foster arranged for him to sing at prestigious parties and industry events, exposing his talents to influential people such as TV host Jay Leno and entertainment mogul Marvin Davis. Meanwhile, new manager Bruce Allen, who by now had replaced Beverly Delich, was put to work persuading Warner's international division to make Bublé a worldwide priority. Jay Durgan, who had worked with Allen on Bryan Adams's career throughout the Eighties when he was an executive with Polygram Records, was now a senior figure at Warners, a fact that certainly didn't hinder the plan.

So it was that Michael did the rounds in the UK, Europe and Asia, copying a policy pioneered by Allen with Bryan Adams. Allen's management partners, Steve Macklam and Sam Feldman, had recently sent Michael's fellow British Columbian, jazz pianist Diana Krall, round the world on a similar pre-release promotional tour, hoping to make the most of radio and television opportunities that were going to be limited compared with more mainstream pop acts. All this, combined with recording duties, would keep Bublé busy for the best part of 18 months.

What had convinced Foster to invest so heavily in Michael? Several factors helped settle the matter once and for all. The first was the stamp of approval Michael received from none other than fellow Canadian singer Paul Anka, a personal friend of David Foster. Indeed, Fifties teen-idol Anka became something of a mentor to Bublé, offering advice and support in equal measure, as well as becoming executive producer for the album.

Anka had begun mentoring Bublé after the two met in 2001 in Las Vegas, where Michael had been opening for chat-show host and stand-up comedian Jay Leno. The day after the show, David Foster had called Michael and told him Paul wanted to meet him. It was a thrill for the young man. "It is an amazing thing to be able to pick up the phone to Paul Anka, who has done this for so long, and is so great at it, and I get to ask him advice on what I should do."

The second and, perhaps, most important factor that turned the *Michael Bublé* project from potential release to reality was the rapport David and Michael quickly developed in the studio, making the entire process an enjoyable and creative time for all concerned.

David regarded one of his most enjoyable studio assignments at that point to have been the *Unforgettable* album he had produced for Natalie Cole, whose father was the late, great jazz giant Nat 'King' Cole. "I remember thinking she was so good with that music because she lived it, she didn't learn it," says Foster. He identified a similar quality in Michael. "He's in a time warp. When everyone else was listening to Nirvana and Metallica, he was listening to Bobby Darin."

There were plenty of initial discussions on what material to record, as Michael is quick to confirm. "We were walking a fine line in the studio. The last thing we wanted to do was a tribute album or a lounge act. We wanted to treat this music with the love and respect it deserves, but the important thing was to capture a spirit and energy and that wasn't confined to any particular musical era. At first we talked about the standards. We wanted some really beautiful tunes. David had this idea to contemporise the album, to try to pay enough respect to the music to make them our style. I think with the tunes we came up with, [the respect] was of the utmost importance."

While Michael Bublé is often viewed as something of a throwback to the days of Frank Sinatra, Dean Martin and Sammy Davis Jr, he wasn't the only artist offering a new take on an old musical style. Robbie Williams, for example, had gone into the Capitol Studios over the course of two weeks in 2001 and emerged with *Swing When You're Winning*, a collection of pop standards that proved a major seller across Europe, earning multi-platinum awards in virtually every country across the continent.

Yet as popular as the album had proved in Europe, it did little or nothing to further or enhance the former Take That singer's reputation in America, where it summarily failed to chart. And Robbie Williams was, at least as far as many were concerned, something of an established star – Michael Bublé wasn't even on the radar at this point in his career.

That said, his combination of musical talent and good looks was fast marking him out as a name to note. The *Philippine Star* labelled him "a finger-snapping hip cat who brings forth the coolest, most romantic sounds imaginable". And his style and fresh-faced image seemed likely to inspire even more column inches: the press purred he had "Matt Dillon's eyebrows and green eyes like Leonardo DiCaprio", and female temperatures were beginning to soar at the mere mention of this new crooner on the block.

There was little argument about using Michael's name as the title of his first album. But there had been controversy about his actual name. The principal disadvantage of the name Bublé was that that it was by no means obvious to Anglophones how it should be pronounced. Philippe Pagès, faced with the same dilemma a decade or so earlier, had chosen his grandmother's name and found worldwide success as Richard Clayderman.

It was suggested that Bublé adopt his mother's maiden name, Santagà. He called Warner Brothers' bluff, asking if the switch would guarantee record sales. The recording company couldn't guarantee that, so Bublé refused. It was, at the least, a line in the sand. The cover featured a close-up profile of his face overlaid with his (real) name, resulting in an intimate yet definitive effect. This was a statement, no doubt about it.

The discussions that Michael, David and Humberto Gatica (David's long-time collaborator and arranger) had over song selection for the album were both exact and detailed. While David and Humberto concentrated on scouring the Great American Songbook for likely titles, Michael, like the former fisherman he was, threw his net out further, recalling the kind of songs his grandfather had introduced him to.

One musical memory, in particular, stood out. Vic Damone's rendition of 'It Had To Be You' had struck a major chord for Michael when, aged 12, Mitch had first played it to him. "I heard this melody wrapped around lyrics that were perfect for each other," he remembered. "A voice that was so beautiful, that hid behind nothing. And it spoke to me because it allowed me to be different. This was a way for me to follow my own beat and not be one of the sheep following what was supposedly edgy and cool."

It was a feeling David Foster could relate to. "Michael, not unlike Natalie Cole or Diana Krall, has lived this music. While everybody else his age was listening to Nirvana and Pearl Jam when they were growing up, Michael was listening to Frank Sinatra, Bobby Darin and Louis Prima and that's what his music reflects. He's not a copy of any of those people, but he's a healthy combination of all those people from that genre."

Like most inexperienced recording artists, Michael was happy to let his producer have the final word on what would eventually appear on the album. "As he's sitting there on his stool, and his head is down and he's thinking, and he's plunking out chords on the piano, I know it sounds funny, but you almost understand what it would be like to watch Beethoven and see that brilliance. It's almost scary just how brilliant he is."

The singer was adamant he didn't want to just do note-for-note copies of any of the material that was selected. "I don't want to be a copycat. What you see is who I am... These guys are the greatest ever. I love to take my favourites – Sinatra, Darin, Sarah Vaughan, the Mills Brothers, Al Martino – and add my own thing."

It was not only songs from yesteryear that provided the material for that debut album, with a number of modern tracks also making the cut. Perhaps the biggest surprise was the inclusion of George Michael's 'Kissing A Fool', which Michael justified by stating, "I don't give a shit if he's gay or straight or he does it with animals – this guy makes good music! I remember dancing to 'Kissing A Fool' with this girl that I really liked. How can anyone *not* enjoy that song?"

From the sessions, conducted over seven months across late 2001 and early 2002 at Chartmaker, Foster's own studio, as well as at the Sony and Paramount studios, a total of 13 songs were eventually selected to make up the final album. (The Japanese and Australian releases boasted one and three bonus tracks respectively.)

Michael opened his major-label debut with 'Fever'. The track is credited to Eddie Cooley and John Davenport – the latter a pseudonym for Otis Blackwell – and was originally an R&B hit for Little Willie John in 1956. Its elevation to something of a standard is down to Peggy Lee, who recorded the first cover version in 1958 and added additional lyrics that have since become an integral part of the song, although she has never been properly credited with her contribution.

Since then 'Fever' has been covered by artists as diverse as Elvis Presley (Otis Blackwell was a regular supplier of material to Elvis), Madonna, The Jam, Ronnie Laws, James Brown, Christina Aguilera and The Doors, so Bublé was in good, if varied, company. And he was clearly undaunted by the fact that Lee's version had remained well-nigh unbeatable. Even Elvis Presley, who'd loved the song so much he'd played it to death while on national service in Germany, had been unable to impress much of his larger-than-life character on it when he recorded it for the album *Elvis Is Back*.

Michael's version owes more to Aguilera than it does Lee. As he says, "I wanted to make it more edgy, more young, a little hip, a little fresh. All we can do really is to love the music and be sincere when singing the words. That's how you make it your own." The different take on an already sexy standard was part of Bublé's masterplan; he didn't want to be just another crooner, a wedding singer who made it big. And above all he didn't want to rip off his idols.

The next track up is 'Moondance', from Irish songwriter Van Morrison's 1970 album of the same name. It was a classic swing track and a natural for Bublé's easy-going style. It would not be the last time he would raid the Irishman's songbook, and he liked the song so much that a live version was one of the Australian release's bonus cuts.

The contrast in eras between Bublé's opening two tracks was an indicator to those discovering him for the first time that he was willing to turn his hand to a number of periods and genres. The standards he chose had been favourites but, as he explained, the newer material had to have that special something as well. "It's a timeless quality."

After George Michael's 'Kissing A Fool' came 'For Once In My Life' from the Motown songbook. Written by Ron Miller and Orlando Murden, the best-known version was that recorded by Stevie Wonder, some months after the original version by Jean DuShon had disappeared without trace. Indeed, it was the failure of DuShon's version that prompted a heated debate between Ron Miller and Motown founder and president Berry Gordy, who felt Miller was forever trying to write middle-of-the-road standards,

The First LP

and that if he wanted to earn a living at songwriting he would be better advised concentrating on the soul and R&B that had made Motown's fortunes in the past. To prove the boss is not always right, 'For Once In My Life' has since become one of the most recorded and covered songs in the entire Motown catalogue!

'How Can You Mend A Broken Heart?' was written by Barry and Robin Gibb (brother Maurice's name was added to the writing credits in 2009) and was originally intended for Andy Williams. But after recording a demo version, The Bee Gees decided to release it themselves, adding it to their 1971 album *Trafalgar* and then releasing it as a single that would go on to top the US chart in August 1971. The song would later attract cover versions by Al Green and Teddy Pendergrass although not, to the best of our knowledge, Andy Williams! Barry and Robin Gibb performed on Michael's version, adding their seal of approval to the up-and-coming artist.

'Summer Wind' provides the album with its first link to the Rat Pack style. The song was written by Henry Mayer and Johnny Mercer and had originally been recorded by Wayne Newton in 1965, but it soon became better known thanks to a cover version by Frank Sinatra the following year.

Having already delved into the Motown songbook, it made sense to pick a song from Kenny Gamble and Leon Huff's Philadelphia International empire, the track chosen being 'You'll Never Find Another Love Like Mine'. Written in 1976 for Lou Rawls, it topped the R&B charts and peaked at number two on the Hot 100, selling over a million copies in the process. Bublé's take earned critics' approval, with one review saluting his decision to turn "the up-tempo hit into a slow jam, with surprising effectiveness".

Michael made a daring choice in 'Crazy Little Thing Called Love', the song that broke Queen in the States to chart-topping effect. Though the original had been first released in 1979, when Bublé was all of four years old, it harked back even further to the heady days of rock 'n' roll's creation. That helped it strike a chord in the former Elvis impersonator's musical memory bank, and his affection for the Fifties-flavoured song was confirmed when it became a staple of his live shows.

The horn-laced swing arrangement contrasted with a genuinely exciting guitar solo to add a new slant to an old favourite. And it may have been no coincidence that his mentor, Paul Anka, followed the same formula the following year when he came out with *Rock Swings* – a whole album of rock classics afforded similar treatment.

New friend Anka also provided 'Put Your Head On My Shoulder', originally written in 1959 and a hit for its composer when it peaked at number two. It also provided a hit for The Lettermen in 1968, but Michael's update proved a much more lushly arranged version of the track. He remembered one of his first crushes when recording the song. "I closed my eyes and pretended that I was singing it to her – that's the sincerity part, just believing in what you're singing." Well, Anka had written his first hit, 'Diana', about his babysitter and it worked for him…

Mexican composer and bandleader Pablo Beltran Ruiz wrote and first recorded 'Quien Sera?' in 1953, but it was the addition of English lyrics by Norman Gimbel and a re-titling of the song to 'Sway' that saw it become a major hit the following year for Dean Martin, making the Top 20 in the US and the Top 10 in the UK. It had subsequently been recorded by Cliff Richard, Rosemary Clooney, Ben E King and Julie London, among others, before Michael added it to his album and repertoire.

The oldest song on the record was 'The Way You Look Tonight', originally written in 1936 by Jerome Kern and Dorothy Fields for the film *Swing Time*. Performed in that movie by Fred Astaire to Ginger Rogers, it would go on to earn an Academy Award for Best Original Song and soon became a standard, being covered by Billie Holiday, Frank Sinatra, Ella Fitzgerald and Andy Williams.

The First LP

'Come Fly With Me' is a song most closely associated with Frank Sinatra, which is not surprising given that composers Sammy Kahn and Jimmy Van Heusen wrote it specifically for him. As well as being the title track to his 1958 album, it became a mainstay of his live performance. But Michael appeared to have no qualms about taking it on.

The final track on the album was the suitably titled 'That's All', written in 1952 by Alan Brandt and Bob Haymes and first recorded by Nat 'King' Cole. It would later be covered by Bobby Darin, Johnny Mathis, Ricky Nelson, Nina Simone and Frank Sinatra among countless others.

Overall, Michael, David and Humberto were extremely pleased with the finished album and the interpretations they had come up with. While the material may have been largely standards, Bublé had brought something else to the party. "The love and the passion I have for singing this music. Since I was a kid, it's had a special place — it's the soundtrack to my life. I think all these songs have something in common. They have a heart and a soul and the challenge of any singer is to connect with those qualities and make them real for the audience."

While the album was being recorded, a subtle change was taking place in the American charts. In among the usual rap and R&B suspects such as Eminem (with the soundtrack to *8 Mile* and *The Eminem Show*) and Jay-Z (*The Blueprint 2*), artists that were more MOR in their make-up were beginning to make a significant impact on the upper echelons of the *Billboard* chart. Leading the way was the pretty face of Norah Jones, whose *Come Away With Me* (which also featured a number of standards in its track list) would sell in excess of 10 million copies in the US and some 20 million worldwide. The market for Michael Bublé was potentially greater than even David Foster had realised.

Promotion, particularly in the form of concerts so that the public could see Michael perform live, and marketing would be crucial to breaking him into the mainstream. But a task that had probably seemed difficult when Michael, David and Humberto began recording had become a whole lot easier by the time the album was ready for release in February 2003.

Michael noticed the change just as his own album was about to drop. "There's enough bad stuff to think about, and it's nice to put on a nice record with romance and nice songs. When I saw [Norah Jones] hitting, I knew music I liked was making a comeback – quality, great melody, nice words and a lot less about image. There's a void in the market. This music isn't better than rap or any other genre. It's just what I love. But I felt that as a consumer I had been left out of the loop a bit – that when I turned on the radio I didn't have a chance to listen to something like Norah Jones or Josh Groban. It's cool that everybody's getting their chance now to be heard."

Nevertheless, Michael's image also undertook a number of subtle changes, courtesy of a shopping trip to Armani and Barney's in New York with Paul Anka. The label also told him to change his diet, dropping the Big Macs that had sustained him for much of his career thus far. Now, Warner Brothers wanted to project a mood of sophistication, a suave appeal rather than a rough-and-ready one. In short, they wanted Michael Buble to appeal to an older, female audience, and for him to look like the kind of man they would want their daughters to marry!

As good as the *Michael Buble* album undoubtedly was, it would take more than a new image to get the point across to the public. Radio would have its place, of course, once an obvious single was identified, but television would play a vital role in promoting the whole Michael Buble experience. Warner Brothers pulled out all the stops in their pursuit of the right outlets; David Foster had ensured that Michael Buble and his eponymous major label debut was the number one priority for 143/Warner Brothers on its February 11, 2003 release.

A fresh-faced Bublé in full flight prior to his major-label debut, 2002. (DENISE TRUSCELLO/WIREIMAGE)

At New York City's Rockefeller Plaza, 2005. (EVAN AGOSTINI/GETTY IMAGES)

Carrying off the prizes at the 2006 Juno Awards held in Halifax, Nova Scotia. (GEORGE PIMENTEL/WIREIMAGE)

Michael and actress/long-time girlfriend Emily Blunt at *The Devil Wears Prada* premiere afterparty, 2006. (EVAN AGOSTINI/GETTY IMAGES)

A model of mutual respect with role-model and mentor Tony Bennett. (KEVIN MAZUR/WIREIMAGE)

In characteristic concert pose on stage in San Jose, California, 2008. (JOHN MEDINA/WIREIMAGE)

Bublé plays the axe hero on NBC's *Today* programme, 2008. (LOUD/GETTY IMAGES)

Manhandling the microphone stand at BMI's 57th Annual Pop Awards, 2009. (KEVIN WINTER/GETTY IMAGES)

The First LP

Yet despite some pre-launch publicity garnered by an appearance at the Super Bowl pre-game show in San Diego, copies of the album were hardly flying off the shelf in the first few days after release. In fact, Michael later revealed that in its first week out, his debut sold all of 41 CDs.

Then, a few days later, Michael secured a three-song appearance on NBC's *Today Show* (on Valentine's Day), also singing with co-host Katie Couric. Later the same day, he crossed the studio to appear in the soap opera *Days Of Our Lives*, playing a lounge singer and performing 'That's All'. The *Today Show* appearance, in particular, was pivotal. As he recalls, "I went on Katie Couric's show, it was Valentine's and I asked her to dance and I sang a song... The next day I sold 15,000 CDs. Wow! I mean can you believe that kind of mileage?" (His website and ad campaigns have, since then, majored on events like Valentine's Day and Mother's Day to encourage gift sales.)

In fact, the day after the Katie Couric show aired, Michael popped into a Times Square music store in order to buy a copy of his own album. "Like the dork I am, I had to buy my own CD. So I walk in and pick up a copy. I'm looking at my picture on the front thinking, 'This is so *cool*.' I take it up to the counter and I hand it over to the cashier sheepishly. The guy looks at it and says, 'Is this you?' I said, 'Well, uh, yeah.' He said, 'This is you?' I said, 'Yeah, it's me.' He said 'It *is* you!' I said 'Yeah, yeah it's me. It's my first record. I had to buy it.' He said, 'You know it's selling pretty good.' I said, 'Oh wow, that's cool.' And then he said, 'By the way, who the fuck *are* you?'"

Universal recognition and acceptance would obviously take time, but at the beginning of March the *Michael Bublé* album made its entrance on the *Billboard* charts, hitting number 47. While it was hardly an earth-shattering entry, this was still a good performance for a relatively new artist (at least, new as far as the record-buying public were concerned) and proof that there was indeed a market for Michael's style of music.

It was a market Michael's new manager, Bruce Allen, was quick to capitalise upon. Another veteran of the Canadian record industry, Allen had been responsible for the management of Bryan Adams and Anne Murray, among others, and used the experience of managing those acts to propel Michael into the limelight. Album sales might have been sluggish, but you'd never have known that, judging from the attendant publicity being generated.

The promotional campaign was aided by a succession of singles, starting with 'How Can You Mend A Broken Heart?' (which was actually released a week before the album in order to create a buzz) – which would make number 22 on the Adult Contemporary Chart. In May came 'Kissing A Fool', which made number 29 on the same chart, and finally 'Sway', which was released in September.

'Sway' performed even better than its predecessors, hitting number 24 on the Adult Contemporary chart, but also making number 22 on the Hot Dance Music & Club Play charts. It also peaked at a phenomenal number three on the Hot Dance Singles, thanks to a remix of the song by the renowned Dutch DJ, Junkie XL. (If the name seems familiar, this was the man who, credited as JXL, turned Elvis Presley's little-known album track, 'A Little Less Conversation', into a worldwide chart-topper in 2002.)

Last but not least, 'Sway' reached the Top 20 in Australia in May 2004, confirming a love affair between Buble and his fans down under that continues to flourish today. Matthew Connors described Buble in an article for *The Australian* as "velvet-voiced, displaying rich, warm tones, immense clarity and near perfect pitch". Two mixes of 'Sway' were duly added to *Michael Buble* for Antipodean consumption.

Despite the acceptance of these three singles on radio, it seemed nothing could lift the album above its Number 47 peak on the *Billboard* charts, and after just ten weeks on the listings it disappeared.

The First LP

But if America had been something of a disappointment sales-wise, salvation was just around the corner in just about every other country in the world. While the UK has been home to many a successful rock act, the British audience could also be relied upon to embrace all kinds of music. If Michael was looking for a spiritual home, then he did not need to look any further than the United Kingdom.

The eventual success Michael Bublé was to enjoy in Europe would be down to a host of people: the man himself, of course, put in a huge effort in making himself available for interviews and tours, abetted by record-company personnel who ensured that as many doors that could be opened remained so when Michael finally arrived. An early convert to the Michael Bublé cause was veteran broadcaster Michael Parkinson, whose radio and television slots had proved of great benefit to a succession of artists over the years, from Billy Connolly to Jamie Cullum. In 2003, it was Michael Bublé's turn to feel the benefit.

"When Michael Parkinson hears a recording he likes, he'll invite the singer on to his show, and that one appearance can transform a career," Michael related the following year. "He did it for Jamie Cullum, Il Divo and Clare Teal and last year he was my champion. If a career can rest on a single appearance like that, it says a lot about how jazz and easy-listening music is constantly overlooked."

The respect was mutual. Parkinson had told his production team he wanted Bublé on the show the moment the singer arrived in the country, having already told them all that Michael's album was the best debut album he had ever heard. The end result was an appearance on Parkinson's television series, which regularly drew some 6.5 million viewers on a Saturday evening, and numerous plays on his weekly Radio 2 show.

Just as it had done in the US, *Michael Bublé* entered the UK chart at its peak position. The difference was that the publicity and promotional work had helped Michael to become a star in the making, and the album hit the ground running. The second highest new entry on the album charts, behind the Elvis Presley compilation *2nd To None*, *Michael Bublé* spent its first week on the chart at number six. It would go on to register 25 weeks on the chart and sell in excess of 600,000 copies, earning Michael a double platinum award from the BPI. It sold well throughout the year, ultimately ranking in the UK's Top 40 albums of the year, ahead of Eminem's *The Eminem Show* – not bad for a virtual unknown!

Nor was the rest of the world about to be left behind. In Australia the album was certified seven-times platinum, while in his native Canada it turned four-times platinum. Among numerous awards was one from the IFPI (International Federation of the Phonographic Industry) to signify over a million sales across Europe. With American sales also eventually topping the million mark, it meant *Michael Bublé* sold well over three million copies worldwide.

Press reaction was generally favourable. *USA Today* reflected that "Bublé's heart belongs to Bobby Darin, Elvis and the young Sinatra", and praised his ability to "channel those American pop-standard icons in a strong tenor voice". Another reviewer said, "throughout the disc it is apparent that Bublé has done his homework and aced the test."

Unsurprisingly, Michael received some of his best press in his Canadian homeland. *Local Ontario* newspaper said he was "touchingly sincere in his renditions of the classics", and Michael told the paper the sincerity in his recordings was deep-rooted in his appreciation of a bygone era.

The success of the album brought many requests for live dates, an area that Michael had paid special attention to during the course of his career. "Showmanship is more important than just singing pretty," he had said, adding, "A lot of people can sing, but I don't see a lot of people putting on a good show. I strive to entertain."

The First LP

His quest to put on a show, rather than just turn up and perform, soon had him marked out as bankable at the box-office. "It's funny, in America, Canada and even Australia now, we never expected this," he said. "We're not rock stars, we play kind of jazzy standards. But our show rocks as much as AC/DC would rock. You have to see the show to understand. This is not Frank Sinatra – it's more like Marilyn Manson – it's a crazy show! But in America it's young people – girls like 13 years old and 25..."

He took care to recruit a band of musicians he could trust and who shared his vision. "I had a blinding ambition, I was ridiculous. [Impersonating himself] 'We're going to sell millions of records, play stadiums, *rahhh!*'"

Alan Chang, who has served as Michael's pianist, musical director and sometime songwriting partner for over a decade, recalled wondering if he was being spun a line as the young man revealed the scope of his ambition. "The first time we went out for drinks, he told me he literally mapped out these eight years. I mean, this was a long time ago! His first record had just come out and he said, 'We'll be doing arenas, doing pop songs, doing Michael Jackson, doing this,' and I was like, 'Yeah, whatever, just buy me another drink'." Neither man was to know, of course, just how much of Michael's dream would come true.

Having spent many of his formative years working with all age groups, Michael knows how to work an audience. And sometimes he'll do just that, with tongue firmly in cheek. In London, at the Café De Paris, he announced, "I think we should skip the next song ['Fever']. I'm protecting you. I do this for a living and I know it can make people horny!"

Michael has the perfect show in mind every time he takes the stage. "It should be a party. It should be music, just me jamming along with my guys in the band, and you just happened to be drinking and hanging out with me. We should be close. You guys should be singing along. I should be in the audience with you. We should be taking pictures of each other."

Michael insisted he couldn't describe a typical fan of his "because there isn't a typical Michael Bublé fan. I know that I have black and white and gay and straight and young and old and rich and poor and everything in-between. This music is something that speaks to everyone. Maybe there are more females than males, but that's about the only way I can categorise."

Sometimes, however, the sheer diversity of his audience can bring its own problems, with Paris as a case in point. "I played this place called the Zenith. I was opening the show. My little sister and her husband had come to see me. I could see her about 20 rows out. I start the show, and all of a sudden, about three songs in, I see this young girl stand up. She's probably about 19 years old, a real good-looking kid. She's singing along and standing on her chair in the front row.

"I watched a woman who was about 60-odd years behind her. The woman tapped her shoulder and said something. I could see the young girl turn back and say something in an aggressive way. And the older woman looked at her and knocked her out! Just punched her on the chin, and I watched this girl drop.

"The next thing you know, people got up and there was a couple of guys fighting. Me and my little sister Crystal locked eyes and I could see her going, 'Hooooaa!' I stopped the show and said, '*Ferme la bouche*, shut your mouth, stop it!' This one guy was starting to get rowdy and I said, 'I'll come and knock you out if you don't shut up.' They probably didn't understand half the things I was saying, but I said, 'I'll walk'. You know what's *really* funny? They didn't kick her out. I looked a few songs later, when everybody was settled down, and they turned and kissed each other on the cheek. Did this make-up thing. I was like, 'Awww, Paris, what lovely people, such warmth.'"

The First LP

Not all of Michael's live shows were quite so volatile, as anyone who has heard *Come Fly With Me* will confirm. Released in March 2004, just as Michael Bublé-fever was beginning to reach around the world, this eight-track live CD (including two new studio tracks) and accompanying 15-track live DVD did sufficient business to make the Top 60 in both the UK (it peaked at number 52) and the US (number 55), earning a gold disc in the UK.

It performed even better in Michael's Canadian homeland, ending up triple platinum, and Australia, where it was a Top 20 fixture on its way to earning another gold disc. And prior to Christmas 2003, there had been a collection of six holiday classics, released as an EP entitled *Let It Snow*, that also did considerable business and hit number 32 on the US charts.

In fact, it was difficult to get away from Michael Bublé as the year progressed, with two of the tracks from his debut album, 'Kissing A Fool' and 'For Once In My Life', turning up in the film *Down With Love*, starring Renée Zellweger and Ewan McGregor. Michael also performed the movie's title track, a duet with Californian singer Holly Palmer, but he was quick to stress this was not intended to herald an acting career or even a conscious move towards Hollywood.

"It's too easy to spread yourself too thin. And soundtracks are a real crapshoot. You just don't know what a movie's going to do. Look at Josh Groban. His music was in *Troy*, which was going to be the biggest movie that ever happened. My music was in *Down With Love*, which was supposed to be this huge movie. Renée Zellweger had just come off *Moulin Rouge*. I enjoyed the movie, but commercially it didn't enjoy the success people thought it would.

"If I can get my music in there," he continued, "I think it's a great thing. They're really just another great form of promotion. I think it's more important for me to actually take the time to tour, to show up and be tangible to my audiences in the twenty-odd countries.

If I start concentrating on acting or soundtracks, I start leaving out valued customers who have been good enough to spend their hard-earned money to buy my product."

Michael might well have put acting and soundtracks out of his mind, but there were others who were quick to capitalise on his new-found fame. In 2001, while trying to earn the $500,000 that David Foster had required for producing his first major-label release, Michael had played the part of singer Van Martin in the low-budget flop *Totally Blonde*, a starring vehicle for Krista Allen. Three years later, in 2004, someone realised that he had become a star in his own right and so lifted the seven tracks featuring Michael and, by means of clever packaging, made it look like an official new release. Although Michael used his website to warn fans not to buy the album, there were plenty who went ahead and did so, expecting the same kind of material they had found on *Michael Bublé*. They were to be disappointed.

There were other disappointments in the pipeline too, not all of them down to the opportunism of others. Instead, Michael was discovering one of the downsides to fame: as a figure in the public eye, *everything* you do is considered in the public domain; make a mistake and the press, in particular, will be quick to bring you down a peg or two.

Early on in his media career, Michael had been frank about his inspiration for pursuing a musical career. "Listen, I would love to tell you that I was this wonderfully smart and full-of-integrity kinda guy. But at the same time, man, I wanted to get *laid*. That was a big part of it! This is why I wanted to be different and why I wanted to have power and fame and money; because I wanted to be attractive to the opposite sex. I'd be lying to you if I didn't say that was a big part of it."

As Michael began to enjoy the power, fame and money his success had brought, there were a succession of female fans ready, willing and eager to help him achieve the other part of his quest. It didn't matter to them that he was in a long-term relationship – more often than not, Michael was in a different continent to Debbie when opportunities arose.

"When I started to enjoy success as a singer, I began to get cocky, because it's easy to lose touch with reality in this business. I would be in a police car being escorted through a crowd of screaming girls, and booze and drugs were all there for me if I wanted it. I had a girlfriend I cared a lot about, but for a while I pushed her aside and said, 'This is my time. I'm going to go and do my thing.' I started to be reckless with people's feelings. I felt I could be rude and say things with no comeback."

While there may have been a shortage of those within the Michael Bublé camp able to bring him back down to earth, the media weren't so unforgiving. A snap of Michael leaving this club with that girl, or that club with this girl, began appearing the tabloids, along with stories of womanising, and these would invariably find their way back home, eventually tearing his girlfriend Debbie Timuss apart. "I was never sleazy. I was never mean to a girl. I was always very upfront. But I'm a regular guy. I am a lad and I did enjoy temptation."

Worse, if at all possible, was still to come, with Michael playing the star card at almost every opportunity. It culminated in a spat with his tour manager during one such tour. "It came to a head when I was on an airplane and was rude to a flight attendant. It wasn't the real me, but I did it. My tour manager, who has worked with much better than me, took me aside. He said, 'Young man. I have met your mother and father. And I know you were raised to be much more classy a person.'

"I thought, 'Yeah, sure.' Then I sat on a five-hour flight and had time to stew. I was so mad, but I had time to think. I prayed, please God help me find my way. I realised he was right and that fame is a fantasy and when it is all gone and fans aren't screaming, what would be left? My family and the girl [Debbie Timuss] who stuck with me for five years when I struggled and had nothing."

If Michael had expected his family to back him automatically in every argument, he was in for a big shock. His mother obviously got to hear about the bust-up and called him soon after. "My mom called me one day and said, 'Did you get better-looking or more charming this year?' And I said, 'I don't know.' And she said, 'No, asshole, you didn't.' They definitely keep me grounded."

While Michael's mother might have been able to pull him around with regard to his general behaviour, his relationship with Debbie would continue to be rocky, even as he attempted to shed his bad-boy image. "You get self-absorbed, not out of evil but out of necessity, surviving that life. Then when you come home, it's hard to break that off and sit down with everyone else, because you're used to doing what you want to do, when you want to do it. You know what? There've been times when I have looked in the mirror and said, 'Get over yourself'."

Whatever problems Michael may have been suffering in his private life, his professional life continued its upward trajectory. On April 4, 2004 at Rexall Place in Edmonton, the Canadian Academy of Recording Arts & Sciences gathered together for its annual Juno Awards ceremony. Michael had received nominations in two categories, Best New Artist and Album of the Year. In the former category he was up against Barlow, Kazzer, Danny Michel and Kinnie Starr, with Michael holding an advantage because, out of all the artists nominated, he was the only one who had made any kind of an international breakthrough. In the latter category he was up against particularly strong opposition, including Celine Dion with *One Heart,* Nelly Furtado and *Folklore,* Sarah McLachlan and *Afterglow,* Nickelback and *The Long Road* and Sam Roberts with *We Were Born In A Flame.*

The First LP

The evening went pretty much as expected for Michael, who walked away with the award for Best New Artist. It was in the Album of the Year category that the real shock came, with guitar-toting rocker Sam Roberts, as unkempt as Michael was suave, overcoming a strong field to win the Best Album statuette. (In fact, Sam won all three categories for which he was nominated on the evening, including Rock Album of the Year and Artist of the Year, so perhaps his success wasn't so great a surprise.)

Michael wasn't disappointed with his evening's work, especially when he thought about the quality of the opposition. To him it was an indication of how far he had come in such a short space of time that he was being mentioned in the same sentence as Celine Dion, Nelly Furtado et al. Besides, if he could keep coming up with the goods, turning out albums that were at least the equal of *Michael Bublé*, then there would undoubtedly be further nominations and further awards to enjoy. Collecting those nominations and awards therefore would depend very much on the success of the follow-up.

While Michael and his team began looking at material for that all-important second album, his profile remained high, thanks to a number of strategic releases. In August the track 'Spider-Man Theme', originally recorded by Michael for his own *BaBalu* album in 2001 (it was included in the 2002 film, but did not make the soundtrack album), was finally lifted as a single in Canada. It became his first charting single there, peaking at number six. The single, remixed extensively by DJ Junkie XL, would also become a major hit in Italy and Australia.

Finally, in the United Kingdom in November 2004, Warner Brothers took the original *Michael Bublé* album and added it to the six-track Christmas EP to create a Special Edition. They were rewarded when the 'new' album entered the charts, spending five weeks on the listing and peaking at number 46.

Though Michael professed himself happy with his eponymous major-label debut at the time of release, the picture changed somewhat as time went by and he did admit to some regrets. "There's things that I wouldn't have done again... I took the arrangements from Billy May and Don Costa, that were done for Frank Sinatra, for the songs 'Come Fly With Me' and 'For Once In My Life'... I *wish* I hadn't done that.

"To take the music and not move ahead. I mean by taking those songs that were arrangements that Sinatra had done, I put myself on a cross. Then everyone was going to say, 'You're trying to be Sinatra'." There had been a battle of wills with David Foster, and the singer had come off second best. "Now we both agree that was, well... I mean, we didn't mean to steal the song, it was meant to be a tribute to the man. But that's experience – we make mistakes and we learn from them."

Even so, Michael's first venture into the music mainstream had seen him emphatically swim rather than sink like a stone. And now there were at least three million fans awaiting his next move, he had every reason to be glad he had dived in.

CHAPTER 4

It's Time

For countless artists in music history and, no doubt, countless more to come, the second album of their career is the most important. It throws up all kinds of possibilities – do you follow exactly the same path as the debut, or do you try and vary things a little, show how you have grown and matured as an artist? If you do exactly the same kind of thing on the second album, will the critics brand you a one-trick pony? If you try and change too much, do you risk alienating the audience you found with your first album?

That was the dilemma facing Michael, David Foster and Humberto Gatica when talk finally got around to a second album, to be released in early 2005. The worldwide sales of *Michael Bublé* had been so impressive there would have undoubtedly been the temptation to produce something that was effectively *Michael Bublé Volume 2*, but Michael had one or two ideas of his own that he wished to put on the table. These, most interestingly, included a composition he had written in conjunction with musical director Alan Chang and Amy Foster-Gillies. As the surname suggests, Amy was the daughter of

David Foster and had already had songs successfully recorded by Josh Groban and Destiny's Child.

There would be other changes too, the most controversial being the introduction of a different producer on a number of tracks. This was another of Michael's suggestions. "I wanted to know what it was like to work with another producer, in another kind of style. I was very worried about this record, because I sold over three million of the first record. And all of a sudden, the pressure's on you. The second record is the most important. The first record's easy. The second record is the most important record in an artist's career. Make or break. I knew that this thing needed to be better than the first, and there is just no way around that. So, I took control."

Happily, the suggestion was warmly welcomed by David Foster. "He was wonderful with me, he allowed me to take more control," Bublé marvelled. "He let me push my weight around a lot more. In songs like 'Home' or 'Feeling Good', that was me pushing, and doing what I felt was necessary as an artist. And then with [producer] Tommy LiPuma, I walked in and I said, 'I want to be able to grow' – to be able to work with someone who has a different style. And David was thrilled about that."

Older by some 13 years than David Foster, and thus in his seventies, Tommy LiPuma has a virtually unmatched pedigree in music production. He specialised in the soul and jazz side of the pop spectrum and, having become a record-business executive, could pick and choose which production jobs he took. He had worked with artists of the calibre of Barbra Streisand, Anita Baker, Natalie Cole, Diana Krall and George Benson, and had received 30 Grammy nominations, winning three times.

The fact he chose to become involved with Bublé was an undoubted feather in the young man's cap. LiPuma's reputation for perfectionism in the studio was something Michael readily confirmed. "Everything just had to be absolutely perfect. Yet, at the same time, David is more of a perfectionist in a way."

The difference, it seemed, was a four-letter word – feel. "Tommy, if there's a little mistake in a song, if the energy is there, he wants to keep it. He'd say, 'Listen, this doesn't *have* to be slick. This doesn't *have* to be perfection. But if the energy is there and it's swinging like crazy and it feels really good, then it's *right*.' Whereas David wanted to have perfection. But I wouldn't allow him. I didn't want it to be too slick. I want it a little bit edgy, a little but more about who I am. I'm not perfect. I'm not slick. I'm passionate, and sometimes it can be a little brash, and that's kind of how I want it."

Never before, perhaps, has an album's title been so apt. Michael's major-label debut had sold in excess of two million copies in the United States, but there was a feeling that *It's Time* would be a watershed moment. It was set for a February 2005 release, like its predecessor, in time to coincide with Valentine's Day. Fans were eager for him to prove whose time it really was – and he didn't disappoint.

As an aside, Michael had apparently originally wanted to call the album *Feeling Good*, after its lead track, but had been overruled by his record company who felt it sounded like a country release. "Listen," was his typically trenchant response, "you can call it *It's Crap* if you like." He reasoned that, "if the title has anything to do with my success or my failure, then I'm in the wrong business."

So *It's Time* it was, the cover an ultra-cool portrait of a besuited Bublé in classic black and white. His smouldering stare into the camera lens exuded sex appeal, while the scrawled initials MB greyed out in the background would increasingly be used as his monogram or trademark. The back sleeve was a variation on the same theme, hands still thrust into pockets and tie rakishly askew. File under simple, stylish and undeniably effective.

The album was set to include Bublé's first original track on a major label, and fans could not wait. 'Home' would show the world that

Michael was not just a covers artist, albeit a popular and successful one. He had something to prove.

UK tabloid *The Sun,* long-time converts to the cause, proclaimed "soon Michael Bublé will be the name on everyone's lips", adding that he had "made jazz popular and, more importantly, cool again". Bublé reiterated through its pages that the return of jazz to the popular-music charts was also due to artists like Norah Jones and Harry Connick Jr, who "showed that there is a huge part of the market for all ages and sexes that like this music".

Michael explained his intentions for the album to Canadian breakfast TV show *Canada AM*: "I think that I wanted it to have continuity with the last one, with good tunes that make people feel comfy and cosy. I wanted there to be a theme running through, which is hope, love, romance, and mostly fun. I mean, this is pop music, you know, the popular music of yesterday and today."

The arrival of the new album sent fans flocking to the shops and online, where it had been made available for download from iTunes the previous week. With the previously mentioned exception of 'Home', the 13 tracks on display drew from the same musical pool as its predecessor. And fans were greeted with a classic opener that let them know Michael Bublé had returned – and how!

The album kicked off with 'Feeling Good', written by Leslie Bricusse and Anthony Newley, a song originally written for the musical *The Roar Of The Greasepaint, The Smell Of The Crowd*. Perhaps of all the songs Michael has tackled, this one has had the most diverse collection of artists recording it at some point in their career, ranging from George Michael, Nina Simone and Frank Sinatra to Muse and The Pussycat Dolls, with an instrumental version coming from legendary jazz saxophonist John Coltrane too – you can't get much more diverse than that!

Bublé's understated opener had no sooner ended than he flew straight into the introduction for the Gershwin brothers' 'A Foggy

Day (In London Town)'. The track suits Michael down to the ground; it was originally made famous in 1937 musical comedy *A Damsel In Distress* starring Fred Astaire, where it was sung by the leading man himself. Later cover versions have been provided by Billie Holiday, Charles Mingus, David Bowie, Petula Clark and Tony Bennett.

The Eddy Arnold and Cindy Walker composition, 'You Don't Know Me', is probably best known thanks to Ray Charles' version originally recorded in 1962. Charles so effectively made the song his own that he was able to revisit it in 2004 with Michael's friend Diana Krall, which may well have been the spur for Michael himself to attempt it.

'Quando Quando Quando' ('When When When' in English) was written in 1962 by Tony Renis and Alberto Testa, with Ervin Drake coming up with the Anglicised lyric that same year. Pat Boone was the first artist to score a hit with it, and it was subsequently definitively covered by Britain's Engelbert Humperdinck. Michael had always envisaged doing the track as a duet and the first singer to be considered was David Foster's teenage protégée, Renée Olstead, whose 2004 album of jazz standards on Warner Brothers, produced by Foster, had met with critical acclaim.

Renée had worked with jazz trumpeter Chris Botti, who would also make an appearance on *It's Time*. Before Michael and Renée actually got to record a note, however, several people connected with the project began to get cold feet due to Renee's age – or, to be more accurate, her youth.

"I had to call her and say, 'Honey, I'm your biggest fan but I can't sing this song to you,'" Michael lamented. "I said, 'You need to understand, you killed it. It's just that you're 15 and I'm 29 years old. I can't look at you and go, 'When will you be mine? Quando, quando, quando.'"

Eventually the name of Nelly Furtado entered the frame. "I wanted someone young, I wanted someone who sings beautifully, and I wanted someone who sells records internationally and can speak Portuguese. So I'm thinking, 'There are people like that everywhere.' And all of a sudden, I thought, 'Nelly Furtado'!"

Fellow Canadian Furtado, a hitmaker since 2000 with songs such as 'I'm Like A Bird' and 'Turn Off The Light', injected a shot of Latin fire into the album. 'Quando, Quando, Quando' actually originated in Italy, but there's more than a hint of passion between the pair that make it different from any other track.

Indeed, Bublé joked during a skit with Nelly at the 2007 Juno Awards in Canada about the reasons behind the duet. "I thought that she was sexy and I thought that maybe I could score with her!" The pair's collaboration got the seal of approval from the man who made the song famous, Engelbert Humperdinck, who said of Michael: "He's got a great talent. I think he's going to be a huge, monster star."

Michael wrote the next track on the album himself. The inspiration for 'Home' came while he was busy touring and doing promotional work, yearning to be back with his family and with longstanding girlfriend, Debbie Timuss. "I was on the road a lot, and I feel really lucky to do what I do, really fortunate. You know, God has blessed me. But at the same time, one of the consequences of success is I miss my family. I really miss them, bad, and I miss my girlfriend, and I wanted to write something. I wanted to write something that everyone can relate to. Not just me, not just a few of us, but, because everyone has had a point in their life that they miss home. And not just home, not their house but the family that makes their home what it is."

Michael revealed the songwriting muse usually struck while he was in the shower, this particular song being the by-product of a bathroom in Rome. "I'm always singing," he explained. "If I do come up with a cool lick, I keep it. I've written so many songs, different kind of songs…"

But Michael was also aware he had to be careful not to flood the album with original material. "That's why I only had one [track on the album]. David Foster called me and said, 'You know Michael, I'm very proud of you, because it's tough to have the self-control to not put on a whole bunch of your original songs. I'm very proud of you for having the respect for your audience, and making sure you don't forget who you are and what got you there.'"

In fact, Bublé insisted, he had made a very conscious decision. "Do I make a record – a self-indulgent, complicated record – that the critics will love, or do I make a record for the people? And I chose to make a record for the people. If you look at the new CD, there's swing, there's a little bit of rock, a little bit of bossa, there's an original. I just refuse to be categorised.

"It's taking my love of standards and adding it to David Foster's pop sensibility. It's almost making a hybrid that doesn't end up in jazz or sitting in pop. That's why I wrote 'Home', so I could cross over to an audience that hadn't been exposed to what I'm doing. When you're working with standards, you don't have to worry about whether there will be any filler on your album. I have to go to the record store and buy too many records for 14 to 15 bucks and I only wanted a song or two. What I love so much about standards is you've got 13 out of 13 songs you want."

Just as his heroes Bobby Darin and Frank Sinatra had their signature tunes, Michael's 'Home' would become one of his, and it would go some way towards silencing his detractors, who pigeonholed him as a man with a great voice but no originality. "This was something that I felt fitted well on the record. Because a lot of the CD is autobiographical, I thought it would help me with some radio and stuff like that. Easier to cross over. And I think it was close enough to my style to not be a strange kind of step away from what I do."

Credited to John Lennon and Paul McCartney, 'Can't Buy Me

Love' is largely the work of McCartney, who wrote the song in Paris in 1964. The Beatles' version was a worldwide chart-topper, although this has not deterred other artists – from jazz legend Ella Fitzgerald (who scored an unexpected UK hit with it) through The Supremes to R&B supergroup Blackstreet – from trying their luck with cover versions.

It proved a surprisingly controversial song choice, however, when the president of Reprise Records, no less, weighed in against its inclusion. But Michael was adamant he would do the song justice. "[He] called and said, 'Get [the track] off the record. It's a travesty to change a Beatles song'," Bublé recalled. "Sure, they wrote the greatest pop songs ever. But I took a song that isn't done that much and made it my own."

'The More I See You' was a major hit in 1966 for Latino singer Chris Montez, but the song was originally written in 1945 by Harry Warren and Mack Gordon and recorded by Dick Haymes for the film *Diamond Horseshoe*. Michael's version was produced by Tommy LiPuma and features some real Hollywood heavyweights as backing musicians. Critics would single it out as a welcome change of pace and feel from the David Foster-produced tracks.

'Save The Last Dance For Me' is most closely associated with Ben E King and The Drifters, who took the Doc Pomus and Mort Shuman-penned song to the top of the US singles chart in 1960. In 1984, Dolly Parton scored a Top five country hit with her version; two decades later, it was time for another.

Thanks to Otis Redding's version, 'Try A Little Tenderness' is almost synonymous with Stax Records, yet the song itself has a much older pedigree. It was written in 1932 by Irving King (a pseudonym used by the songwriting team of James Campbell and Reginald Connelly) and Harry M Woods, and was initially recorded by The Ray Noble Orchestra, with Val Rosling on vocals, three decades before Redding's definitive revamp.

It's Time

The hit Motown team of Brian Holland, Lamont Dozier and Eddie Holland wrote 'How Sweet It Is (To Be Loved By You)' for Marvin Gaye in 1964. It was subsequently covered by fellow Motown act Junior Walker & The All Stars and, later, James Taylor, in whose hands it became a modern soft-rock standard.

Leon Russell's 'A Song For You' has been covered by Donny Hathaway, Cher, Aretha Franklin, Nancy Wilson and The Carpenters, with Andy Williams also scoring a minor US hit with it in 1971. Michael's version features a trumpet solo from the aforementioned 'smooth jazz' star Chris Botti, who received a 'featuring' credit for his trouble. (Michael Bolton would later include Botti on an album of duets, suggesting that imitation is the sincerest form of flattery.)

'I've Got You Under My Skin' was written in 1936 by Cole Porter, and would later become something of a signature tune for Frank Sinatra. Frank had first sung the song in 1946, but the most successful version of the song was that by Frankie Valli & The Four Seasons, who hit the US Top 10 and UK Top 20 with it in 1966.

The final song on the album was 'You And I', written by Stevie Wonder and débuted on his *Talking Book* album in 1972. Although never released as a single in its own right, it has become one of the Motown legend's most famous ballads. Wonder was supposed to contribute a harmonica solo to Michael's version but didn't make it to the session, so the idea was shelved. Even so, this was another seal of approval – Stevie had obviously heard the previous album's 'For Once In My Life', but that brassy late-1968 song was miles away from this more reflective effort.

Taken as a whole, *It's Time* didn't stray too far from the overall sound of *Michael Bublé*. It would certainly find favour with the three million who had bought his first album, but Michael was more than happy with the finished article, confident that it would enable him to expand his still-growing audience.

"I would say it's much better. I think it shows maturity, I think it's far more exciting, far less obvious and it's a much better representation of who I am. I mean, it's just a far better record. And I'm not saying that the first one was shit, you know? I'm very proud of the first record. I just think I sound better, and sang much better and sang with more confidence, more feeling [on *It's Time*]."

Much of this, he believed, was to do with controlling what songs were chosen and the tempo at which they were sung – in short, the feel. He illustrated this with 'Quando Quando Quando'. "They wanted to do it in a quick kind of way. And I just thought, 'No possible way I'm gonna do this!' I thought it was a pretty song with nice lyrics, and I thought, 'Why can't it be *elegant*? Why can't I put a nice bossa to it, and have someone like Nelly Furtado come in and give it an elegant, sexy feel, instead of just doing a recreation?' I wanted to do a reinvention. I wanted to give it a rebirth, and make it mine. Again, take a song like 'Can't Buy Me Love'. A lot of people don't even know what song it is because it's completely different.

"But I was also careful to have respect for my audience, for the people who bought the record, and to have a Nelson Riddle arrangement on there with 'I've Got You Under My Skin', just to keep continuity with the first record. So, I couldn't have been more pleased with this record. It's funny, you know. I called my manager when I was finished and I said, 'Bruce, I'm finished and I've made a great record for you. I can't tell you how thrilled I am with this. If I sell ten copies, I don't care, because I did something that I'm proud of.' And he said, 'Oh, that's just *great*! That's what you love to hear – an artist who loves his own record, and then we only sell ten copies!'"

With *It's Time*, Michael had effectively carved a niche market for himself. There had been artists who had covered standards in the past, but none had managed to do it quite as successfully. It helped, of course, that Bublé had boy-band-style good looks, but that alone would not have been able to sustain a career, let alone grow one. Even having a strong, professional team around him would not have been enough, since music history is littered with acts who, despite the back-up, couldn't quite live up to the hype. For Michael Bublé, it was more a case of being the right man in the right place at the right time. And with the right song selection.

"I want to be tangible to my audience. I've performed in everything from small clubs to major concert halls. It's been a tremendous confidence builder, which I think is reflected in the performances on my new album, and it gave me a chance to try out some of the new material and find out what worked. I think the sessions really benefited from [my] having come straight off the road into the studio. Between David, Humberto Gatica and I, we were fanatical about getting just the right balance of songs to put on the record. There may be better pop singers and jazz singers out there, but nobody has as much passion for this music as I do – and I think you can hear that on the record."

Up to this point in his career, Michael had often been linked with Frank Sinatra, many claiming the young Canadian was effectively Sinatra's heir. Indeed, his albums were released through Reprise, the label that Frank Sinatra founded. While the comparison was often complimentary, Michael was quick to show that he had other strings to his bow. "I think people expect me to come out in a tuxedo smoking a cigar with a Scotch in my hand, saying, 'It's a pleasure to be here – how did you all get in my room?' But I'm young, I'm immature, I'm a punk, I'm everything that a good young man should be."

He went on to cite Sinatra's album *Live At The Sands* as the standard to which he aspired. "Does it get any better? I don't think so. Here we have Sinatra in his prime. Just hear his tone, his vibrato, and picture his cocksure swagger as he's walking on stage and you will understand why there will never be another like him. Listening to this made me learn that I could never try to imitate him, and, to be honest, Elvis Presley and Bryan Adams have been far bigger influences. Frank was just a man with a great voice who sang the songs I liked."

When he recorded 'I've Got You Under My Skin', a song inextricably linked to Sinatra, Michael knew that recording it would have the critics sharpening their pencils with glee, but he ploughed on regardless. Sure enough, some of Michael's detractors used the track as a stick to beat him with. The *LA Times* labelled it "karaoke", adding that it was only included to "please the traditionalists in Bublé's audience". However, *People* magazine begged to differ, proclaiming that Michael performed it "with such snappy, devil-may-care flair that you'll swear he was born in another time".

The album received a more measured response than his debut, with his audience and critics seemingly wanting different things from Michael. Some critics were harsh on the record upon its release, many urging Michael to ditch the covers. The *LA Times* said that the album was "a collection that displays an extraordinary amount of vocal skill while almost never revealing the heart and soul of the singer". The *Winnipeg Sun* added, "Imitation may be the sincerest form of flattery – but when it comes to music, it's also the sincerest form of futility." Britain's *Word* magazine put it this way: "There is nothing wrong with a bit of retro, but when you play it too safe you get nothing more than repro. It would be good to hear some emotional release."

But Bublé dismissed his detractors, telling the *Herald Sun Melbourne* that he almost relished it, even admitting to googling himself! "The worse the reviews, the better," he said. "I get a kick out of it. I like when they get really nasty. And it has nothing to do with the music a lot of the time – it's, 'I hate his hair, he is ugly' – I *love* those! I read them to my mum, she gets really pissed off. I know there are great reviews; I wish I was into reading those, but I'm not."

It's Time

It's Time was about slowly phasing in original content while keeping in mind what was important – the fans, and what they wanted. And it seemed they wanted Bublé stamping his mark on the classics.

Michael was at pains to get that message across: "I get upset when I see other artists who are too self-indulgent: it can ruin a career when it becomes about you. It's not about you. It's about people who go to work in a factory and save up so they can buy your CD for their wife or their girlfriend or themselves. You have to remember you're making a record for people – not for yourself, not for critics, not for record executives."

He was delighted when Tom Dreesen, a stand-up comedian who worked with Sinatra for 17 years as an opening act, told him he was the only performer he had seen who was capable of keeping the torch going. Another fan was a Sinatra contemporary who, happily, was also still very much around. Over to Michael…

"I just watched Tony Bennett on television and the interviewer said, 'Tony, of all these young kids coming up do you have a favourite?' He said, 'No, I can't say that I do,' then he stopped and said, 'Well, yes, I do actually, it's Michael Bublé.' He said he hadn't seen 'anything like it since the young Sinatra', and he said, 'He can sing anything and make it his own, and I'm a huge fan.' A million critics can say I suck – but to hear Tony Bennett say that, I know I'm doing the right thing."

Michael had often mentioned Tony's name as one of the inspirations for his own career, and to now hear one of his heroes giving out praise in equal measure meant the world. The pair finally met up when both were on tour in Italy.

"People like Tony are idols of mine. He is the coolest dude. He is one of the few men I have idolised who haven't disappointed me when I finally met them. I was in Italy… in a hotel room and he called me and said, 'We're staying in the same hotel. Come down for dinner.' I went down and he said, 'Michael, I'm so proud of you keeping this music alive. I am so excited to see that the young people in Italy are getting it because the record company never broke me back here!' I am very proud to say that he is my friend and my mentor."

Michael used the opportunity to ask for a few pointers on career longevity. "As he came to my show I asked him, 'You have such a great long career', and he said, 'I never pretended to be something I wasn't. And through the years I've been popular and unpopular, style comes in and out, but I continue to sing the great songs and they live forever.' I really believe that…"

Another treasured memory of Italy for Michael was taking his grandfather, Mitch, back to his ancestral homeland. Ever since the first album he had been asking Michael, "Are you famous in Italy yet?", and the chance for the younger man to show he had 'cracked it' in the land of their forefathers proved too strong to resist. But then the roles curiously reversed. "We got off the plane," Michael recalled, "and he turned into a 14-year-old."

With the experience of promoting the first album still very much in mind, the same kind of campaign was envisaged when *It's Time* was promoted to the media. The difference this time around was that, instead of having to chase interviews and appearances, the people behind the campaign could pick and choose which media outlets they went for. Instead of accepting every request, the Michael Bublé camp could now turn down interviews and appearances.

That is not to say Michael was on his way to becoming a male diva, or thought himself too aloof to talk to the media and therefore his fans, but there were so many requests for his time that it would have been physically impossible to accommodate all of them. Instead, media requests were effectively screened; those with the highest circulation or number of viewers, as well as those who had been on board the Bublé bandwagon from day one, would take precedence.

Those fortunate enough to get an interview with Michael were seldom disappointed as he could always be relied upon to come up with the goods. As his itinerary began to fill up, he complained to one interviewer that he felt the record company was treating him "like a monkey They feed me pellets and I do the show. When I hang up from you, they'll come and take the monkey, put him on an airplane and fly him to Paris. I like wearing the nice suits, but they put a little hole in the bum so my tail can stick out.

"I live in a fantasy world," Bublé continued. "Nonetheless, I think I can enjoy it if I keep in mind that it's not real life. Onstage you have to be one person, bigger than life, and it's important to turn that off when you get offstage. Be a quiet guy who loves his family. You can stick the monkey on the road for two years, but if you put the monkey's family with him he'll just keep going. Listen to me – the monkey likes it!"

It's Time proved to be successful enough to keep Michael in monkey nuts for the rest of his life. Initially available on download for a week on iTunes, the physical release came on February 15, 2005. A week later it entered the *Billboard* chart at number seven and would go on to register nearly two years on the listings. It eventually went triple platinum with sales just shy of three million, proof that Michael had successfully cracked the American market. Even more impressive was the album's performance on the *Billboard* Jazz Chart, where it spent 104 weeks, including an unprecedented 78 weeks at the summit. Not surprisingly, *It's Time* was named the top jazz album for both 2005 and 2006 by the US trade paper.

The American campaign was eventually centred around the release of three singles: 'Feeling Good', 'Home' and 'Save The Last Dance For Me'. 'Feeling Good' was used in the promotional commercials for ESPN's television coverage of the 2005 World Series of Poker Tournament, although the single made little or no headway in the chart despite the exposure such coverage afforded. However, for some reason it proved immensely popular in Poland, proof that Michael was able to break into new markets with his music! France was also a priority with the record company, Michael spending a significant amount of his time there.

The semi-autobiographical 'Home' was a minor hit, making Number 72 on the *Billboard* Hot 100 (although it did make it all the way to the top on the Hot Adult Contemporary Tracks chart) and Number 39 in the UK, where it was his singles chart debut.

Two years later, in a move that pleased Michael, top Irish vocal group Westlife recorded a cover version of 'Home'. The master interpreter of other people's material had written a song that others wanted to record! The number was reportedly hand-picked by music mogul Simon Cowell, who would later show his admiration for Michael with regular invites to his UK music talent show *The X Factor*.

Westlife's version would reach number three in the UK, while in the US, country star Blake Shelton also tried his hand at the song. His version charted just outside the US Top 40 but topped the country charts in February 2008. Michael was beginning to receive respect as a songwriter, a development he could scarcely have foreseen.

As previously mentioned, Michael co-wrote the track with pianist Alan Chang and David Foster's daughter Amy Foster-Gillies. Chang remembers the moment that Bublé came to him with the concept for the song. "He had the first few lines of the song written when he came to soundcheck one day. He was expressing the sentiment we've all felt of wanting to be home after being gone for a long period of time. When I first heard what he had to say, I felt it might be too much of a complaint, especially since it was about being stuck in Europe, where we happened to be. I thought to myself, 'Oh great, complain about being stuck in Europe.' But I thought basically it was a good idea, so I figured I'd just go with it and try to come up with music that would fit that theme."

Foster-Gillies didn't subscribe to the Europe-bashing theme either, instead claiming: "I really wrote the lyrics about just the difficulties of being away from home. I think it worked out really nice and balanced between sort of longing to be home but still knowing there is a gratefulness about where he is."

The final single to be lifted from the album, 'Save The Last Dance For Me', barely cracked the Hot 100, peaking one place inside at number 99, but it did make number five on the Hot Adult Contemporary Tracks chart, a listing Michael had pretty much made his own. Yet singles success was never the main priority – albums and the lucrative touring market were where the real action was to be found.

Meanwhile, *It's Time* continued its relentless assault on the charts around the world. Released in the UK a week ahead of America, it again entered the chart at its peak position. This time, it was the third highest new entry on the chart behind Athlete's *Tourist* (which was number one) and Feeder's *Pushing The Senses* at number two. Michael and *It's Time* eased into the chart at number four and would ultimately prove to be the biggest winner. *It's Time* surpassed both *Tourist* (29 weeks and platinum) and *Pushing The Senses* (15 weeks and gold) in terms of staying power and total sales, going on to register a total of 44 weeks on the chart and equalling its predecessor in earning Michael a double platinum award from the British Phonographic Industry.

An already groaning mantelpiece would have to find room for more awards over the coming months, the album eventually being certified three-times platinum in the US, five-times platinum in Australia (where total sales exceeded 350,000 copies and he was now capable of selling out the Sydney Opera House), six-times platinum in Canada (sales in excess of 600,000), twice platinum in Germany (400,000 sales) and eight-times platinum in Italy (620,000 sales). Not surprisingly, the IFPI would eventually honour Michael with a double Platinum Europe award, signifying total European sales in excess of two million copies.

It's Time would go on to shift some six million copies worldwide, taking Michael's cumulative sales towards the ten million mark – an extremely impressive figure in such a short space of time. But it was the various annual awards ceremonies which confirmed that Michael had made the significant step from singer-with-potential to successful artist in his own right.

Michael's major successes came in Canada's Juno Awards, held in Halifax in Nova Scotia on April 2, 2006, although there was to be some controversy during the course of the evening. Michael had received a total of five nominations from his peers in the Canadian industry: Pop Album and Album of the Year for *It's Time*; Single of the Year for 'Home'; Artist of the Year; and Juno Fan Choice Award. Despite strong competition from fellow British Columbian Diana Krall in the Artist of the Year category, Michael's international success in particular ensured that he walked away with the trophy.

In the Album of the Year category, *It's Time* saw off competition from Nickelback (*All The Right Reasons*), Diana Krall (*Christmas Songs*), Kalan Porter (*219 Days*) and Rex Goudie (*Under The Lights*) to win the award. As Pop Album of the Year, it repeated its success over Kalan Porter, also beating eponymous albums from Boom Desjardins and Jann Arden, and *These Old Charms* by Theresa Sokyrka.

Michael's only disappointment on the night came in the Fan Choice category. Voted for by music fans from all across Canada, Michael was beaten on the night by pop-punk band Simple Plan, who also managed to overcome Diana Krall, Nickelback and Celine Dion – so he was in exceptional company.

But the controversy came with the award of the Single of the Year category. The field that year was a particularly strong one, with Michael up against Bedouin Soundclash and 'When The Night Feels

My Song', Feist and 'Inside And Out', k-os and 'Man I Used To Be' and Nickelback with 'Photograph'.

It is taken as read that no-one other than the event organisers knows who has won in any category until it is announced from the stage on the evening. It adds to the drama and makes for better television. So there would have been many millions among the viewers watching the ceremony at home who would have been surprised when the show cut away for a break midway through the ceremony. A commercial then ran congratulating Michael on his success in winning Single of the Year, at least half an hour before the result was announced!

After the show both CTV, the national broadcaster, and Warner Brothers Canada were quick to stress that they had not had prior warning or notice of Michael's win in the category. It was, they revealed, common practice for the record companies to prepare a series of commercials to be used in the event that an artist win in a particular category – no doubt Roadrunner had prepared a commercial congratulating Nickelback for 'Photograph'.

Eventually CTV also confirmed that the airing of the commercial was a control-room error, broadcast instead of another congratulating an earlier winner! Fortunately there was little or no fallout from the incident, most post-show commentators concentrating on a series of gaffes made by host Pamela Anderson.

Having been fêted by the Canadian music industry, Michael Bublé also received the fillip of a nomination for Best Traditional Pop Vocal Album category at the Grammy Awards. Here Michael was up against the strongest possible competition, including Tony Bennett (who had effectively made the category his own, with no fewer than ten wins since the award was introduced in 1992) with *The Art Of Romance*, Johnny Mathis and *Isn't It Romantic*, Carly Simon and *Moonlight Serenade,* and Rod Stewart with *The Great American Songbook Volume IV*. Stewart had won the previous year with his third volume of song classics, but on the night Tony Bennett collected the award. *It's Time* may have been an apt title, but Michael would have to wait a little longer for his time to come at the Grammy Awards.

In fact, it was just one year later that Michael garnered another nomination in the same category for his album *Caught In The Act,* although this time the controversy arose before the ceremony – and was entirely of Michael's own making. The album itself, released in July 2005, was similar in format to *Come Fly With Me*: an eight-track CD coupled with a 19-track DVD derived from his performances for the PBS television special *Great Performances* and a live show at the Wiltern Theater in Los Angeles. Just as with *Come Fly With Me*, the album package proved a popular buy among his existing fans, selling sufficient quantities to reach the *Billboard* Top 200 (it peaked at number 82), the *Billboard* Jazz Chart (number two) and the UK album chart, where it reached number 25 and earned gold status.

Rather than bask in the glow of his second consecutive nomination, an accolade in its own right, Michael used it as an opportunity to take a pop at the whole ceremony. The sheer length of the event, with no fewer than 109 awards handed out on the evening, meant that it was not physically possible to televise the entire show; there would be some awards that would be presented during the dinner, where only the attendees would be present to see who won what. Michael was less than comfortable with that.

"They give away our best traditional pop award at a dinner before the Grammys. I just think that's bullshit. I think it's absolute crap. Our category is now selling way too many records to be given away at a dinner before, so I'm just not going to show up. Why should I go to the Grammys? Because I'll lose… They might as well have already scratched Tony Bennett's name into the damn thing. I'm not going. I'm on that record that I'm going to lose to, and it'll be the second year in a row that I've lost. I'm not going to go."

Such an outburst was almost without precedent. As Michael said, he certainly did appear on Tony Bennett's album *Duets: An American Classic* (the pair performed 'Just In Time', originally a hit for Tony in 1956), but no album has a divine right to win. Besides, the competition in the category was particularly strong that year, with Michael also being up against Sarah McLachlan's *Wintersong*, Bette Midler's *Sings The Peggy Lee Songbook* and Smokey Robinson's *Timeless Love*. Not one of the other artists made any complaint about the strength of the competition or the fact that the ceremony, should they win, would not feature in the televised section of the show. It was, at the very least, a display of civility from his opponents that Michael would have been well advised to take on board.

In the event, Michael did attend the show and, just as he had predicted, Tony Bennett won the award for the tenth time. While Michael would have undoubtedly had many opportunities to apologise personally to Tony for his outburst, neither artist has chosen to make the nature of the apology – if it was offered – public. But that did not stop the media from leaping on this uncharacteristic outburst from Michael, especially as he was seen to be making disparaging comments about a man he publicly acknowledged as an idol.

"It was devastating. I'm not exaggerating, I shook for two days," he later recalled. "But if I could go back I'd have said the exact same thing, just not in such an ineloquent way. This thing will haunt me for the next 20 years. But what the hell... Put it in context. I just said that rap, R&B and rock all get their chance to get shown on the Grammys, how could this music not? I embarrassed myself by using the words I used."

Even Michael was surprised at the level of criticism he received after the event, especially since the media had so firmly been on his side while he was climbing the steps of success. "It sucks when critics don't like you. I don't care who you are or what artists say, but you do care when critics don't like you. Fear of failure drives me. I look at my dad and grandpa and I hope I can be half as successful as they are. They are regular blue-collar guys whose families love them to death. They are loved unconditionally by me and their relatives. One day this may all go away. If it does, I have what's important."

And, at a time when the criticism was at its most barbed, what was important was the unconditional love and affection not only from his family but also from his quickly growing fan base. Eating dinner while waiting to see whether or not you had won an award didn't hold anywhere near as much appeal for Michael as getting out on the road and meeting his fans face to face.

So he spent month after month touring the globe, performing sellout shows to critical acclaim, even if there were additional problems to contend with along the way, including the eventual break-up of his relationship with Debbie Timuss in November 2005. As will be covered in more detail in chapter seven, the pair went their separate ways, despite having become engaged the year before, the apparent reason being Michael's admitted inability to stay faithful to the girl who had shared his early struggles.

The never-ending round of tours and promotional work meant Michael seldom had an opportunity to enjoy his success, but he took as inspiration the experiences of other performers he spoke to along the way. "I talked to Tony Bennett and said, 'Is it OK if I don't smell of roses as often as I should?' He told me he had his first hit and went on holiday. He said, 'I was lackadaisical and I didn't have another number one hit for five or six years. Never again did I get complacent.'"

The release of *It's Time* coincided with that of Gwen Stefani's *LAMB* [*Love Angel Music Baby*]. "I sat with this woman on 16 different airplanes," Michael recalled, using her as an example of effective self-promotion. "Never spoke to her, never met her. I was busting my gut, doing all this promo, and so was she. And look at her success. People wonder why records don't work – Gwen Stefani was up for the challenge. She was probably tired and grumpy, but you can't just make a record these days and hope radio will play it and do all the work for you. It's not going to happen."

So Michael settled into a routine that meant doing all the work possible. "I did three music videos in about three days. The next morning after the last video, I got on an airplane and I flew to France, I got there about six o'clock in the morning, Paris time, went to a TV show, did press all day." Michael even surpassed himself later on when he finished a concert date in Australia, jumped on a plane back to France, did another television show and then returned to Australia to continue the tour!

Such dedication and endeavour certainly brought the rewards, but with it, hand in hand, came expectation as thoughts began to turn to the third Michael Bublé album. If *It's Time* was an important album in Michael's career, then the next one was going to be absolutely vital.

CHAPTER 5

Call Me Irresponsible

"At no point have I celebrated the success of the last two records and nor will I celebrate the success of this one, if it's successful," Michael Bublé announced shortly before *Call Me Irresponsible* was released to an expectant public on the first day of May 2007. "The second it comes out I'll go to work, I'll tour. And my mind is already on the next record. Coming up with great ideas."

It was this continual assessment of his career and understanding of his audience that kept Michael's star in the ascendancy. "With this album, I said to David over and over again, 'Growth without alienation.' Give the audience the odd bit of cheese, but let's not step over the line. Foster's a genius like I'll never be, but his instinct is to play safe, give the audience what they know they want, and I want to take it to another level. Growth without alienation. If we just keep giving them the same thing, why will they keep buying it?"

Bublé admitted to the fear his latest creation might not surpass its two major-label predecessors. "It had to show growth without alienating anyone. So I sat there from the very beginning and came up with the songs, put together the skeleton, and thought about what arrangers I would hire. I even ended up at the mastering session, which artists rarely attend. I wanted to be involved in every aspect because I wanted it to be conceptually beautiful."

And high expectations brought pressure along with them. "I wake up some mornings and think God has blessed me, I'm very good at what I do. And the next morning I think, 'My God, I'm not fooling anyone, I'm a complete fraud.' I'm insecure and my confidence goes back and forth; one day I'm the king, the next I'm a pauper. It's a tough business. It's a slog, but it's work that I love. It's funny, though, with this record I wanted to take more risks. I think I've made it eccentric and, at the same time, palatable."

The *Ottawa Citizen* previewed the release enthusiastically: "Another Bublé disc, another round of *tsk-tsk*-ing from Sinatra purists – but maybe now's the time to wave the white flag." Time would tell if Michael would silence his critics, but he admitted to the Associated Press that he arrived at the album with a somewhat tempered view of his success after five years at the top in the industry. "In certain ways I am more confident and in other ways I am far more humble. I realise I have made a lot of mistakes and done things wrong. I didn't come in with the same kind of desperation that I may have had on the first or second record. I didn't come in thinking, 'Oh God, please. I hope this does well because I have nothing else and I worked so hard at this.' I have come to the point now where I am really allowing myself to enjoy it – *really* enjoy it."

The worldwide success of *Michael Bublé* and *It's Time* had created new problems for Michael and his team to contend with. A new album was now considered an event, not just in his Canadian homeland but all around the world, with his growing fanbase in America, Britain and Australia, in particular, having surpassed even his wildest expectations. Every aspect of the forthcoming album was going to be important, and Michael wanted to be involved in every decision.

While Bublé had a very clear idea about the songs he wanted to include on the album, he was equally certain about those he *didn't* want. "David [Foster] wanted me to do Chris De Burgh's 'Lady In Red' on this album. I said, 'David, I love you man, but I *cannot* go there. Far too obvious. I can't do something just because it's popular.

"I have my own cheesy ideas, but there's a line my instincts say I must not cross. I want to stick around, and that means pleasing, but, even as you sing schmaltz, you have to develop, you have to be fresh, but you have to do it without losing your audience, by taking them with you. We definitely have a great working relationship where I think I interfere just enough. I mean, David is the greatest producer in the world. He and Humberto [Gatica, co-producer] are both so amazing. I couldn't do it without them."

If *It's Time* had been a watershed release for Michael, then *Call Me Irresponsible* would see him come of age. He would include more of his original material on the record, a move that would ultimately land him his first Grammy. What was more, he was also confident enough to insist on singing each song live instead of recording multiple takes and splicing them together for a pristine version, as on the two previous albums. "David and I sometimes go to war over our sense of style," he admitted. "I like things to be a little more loose and dirty, and he likes things to be perfect."

The album's release was scheduled for May 2007 and, with more than two years having elapsed since *It's Time*, the anticipation was building. The 13 tracks on *Call Me Irresponsible* were designed to show how far Michael had travelled over the past couple of years, and there was a particular eagerness to hear his two co-written efforts, titled 'Everything' and 'Lost'.

Both songs drew on Michael's own personal experiences for their inspiration. 'Lost' was an affectionate look back to his now-ended eight-year relationship with Debbie Timuss. "It's an anthem for star-crossed lovers," its writer explained. "Sometimes relationships don't work out because love isn't enough, but that doesn't mean you have to discard the person. There is a way to end a relationship and still be there when they need you. That's basically what it's about."

As might have been expected, the development of the song had been far from straightforward. "I'd written bits of lyrics in Melbourne and put it away. I was literally getting choked up. I took it to Jann [Arden, fellow Canadian songwriter], she came up with 'We'll get lost together', and it was perfect. I didn't want it to be sad, I didn't want people to hear it and slash their wrists. I wanted it to be uplifting."

In contrast, 'Everything' was inspired by a new lady in his life, British actress Emily Blunt. The pair had met backstage at the Australian television Logie Awards in 2005 and their romance proceeded so far and so fast that, at the time of the album's release, the pair were happily ensconced in a newly built $2.2 million mansion Emily had bought in Vancouver.

"I wrote 'Everything' about the great happiness of real love," her house guest explained, "but at the same time I was making a statement about the world. We're living in really crazy times, and I wanted to say that no matter what's happening, this person in my life is what really makes it worthwhile."

As it turned out, 'Everything' was the only track on the album not produced by what the *Toronto Star* described as "the tried-and-true production team of David Foster and Humberto Gatica". Canadian Bob Rock brought to the studio the experience of having worked with rock acts such as Bon Jovi, Bryan Adams and Metallica, and the result was something different. (Perhaps what drew the two together was their shared love of ice hockey: in 2008, Rock would supervise the competition for a new theme to TV's popular *Hockey Night In Canada* programme… and no, Michael *didn't* enter!)

Call Me Irresponsible kicked off with the aptly titled 'The Best Is Yet To Come'. Like many of the songs Michael has sung or recorded, it is most closely associated with Frank Sinatra, thanks to his 1964 recording with the Count Basie Orchestra – indeed, its title actually adorns Sinatra's tombstone. Yet it was actually written by Cy Coleman and Carolyn Leigh for Tony Bennett.

While many might think Michael was making a rod for his own back by recording another song indelibly linked to Ol' Blue Eyes, he was philosophical about the constant comparisons. "It was to be expected," he smiled. "I am singing a genre of music that people are very protective of. I am being compared to the greatest vocalist of all time.

"Someone asked me the other day, 'Do you get upset when people say you are the young Frank Sinatra?' It doesn't upset me. It is a huge compliment, but it is false. There will never be another Frank Sinatra. I never wanted to be another Frank Sinatra. I only wanted to be Michael Bublé."

Michael was also defiant about the association with Tony Bennett, whose influence on his career is well documented. "I believe [my version is] far more aggressive – and a different take [than Bennett's]," he told the *Montreal Gazette* of 'The Best Is Yet To Come'. "At some point I have to somehow be strong enough and I have to have the integrity to sort of say, 'You know what? I make these songs my own and I can't worry about what others have done.'"

Fewer listeners would have been familiar with 'It Had Better Be Tonight (Meglio Stasera)'. The song originated in the 1963 film *The Pink Panther*, written by Henry Mancini (music), Franco Migliacci (Italian lyrics) and Johnny Mercer (English lyrics). It was performed in the film by singer, actress and model Fran Jeffries. Though the song was not his personal choice, Michael knew Mancini's background and was happy to be associated with such a prolific and respected composer. The song was remixed for the clubs by Eddie Amador and became a surprise dancefloor success.

The idea of recording 'Me And Mrs Jones' came up at dinner one night, when Foster pitched the smouldering soul hit about a man's affair with a married woman to Bublé. He didn't even know the song, which Billy Paul had taken to number one on the national *Billboard* chart in 1972, but girlfriend Emily proclaimed, "Oh, my God, this is *wonderful!*" They went home, put it on an iPod and Bublé glumly concluded, "It sucks." But after six or seven more listenings, he started to appreciate the melody and, later, the lyrics in a "sexy yet kitschy" way.

When, while recording it, Foster suggested adding a female voice, Bublé recommended his girlfriend. The producer auditioned her and she got the part, completing her contribution in one take. But every time the recording was aired in company, Blunt would turn down her vocals. "I don't usually say anything," Bublé said. "She cringes easily." The influential *New York Times* approved of the result, describing it as "an impassioned, almost frighteningly persuasive ode to adultery". Michael himself has introduced it thus: "I'd like to dedicate this song to all the husbands and wives in the audience who may or may not be cheating on each other!"

Leonard Cohen's 'I'm Your Man', title track of a 1988 album, was a slightly left-field choice. Although a fellow Canadian, few would have identified the reclusive singer-songwriter and poet as a Bublé inspiration. But Michael assured the *Montreal Gazette*, "I've always loved Leonard Cohen", adding, "What a great way to be able to take this slow-burning, sexy, dark song into my world."

His admiration and respect for Cohen led him to ring the man himself ahead of interpreting his song: "I said to him, 'I'm afraid to do the track live.' He said, 'Why are you afraid?' And I said, 'Well, Leonard, you wrote such a sexy song, I'm afraid the men are going to throw their underpants at me!' And Leonard said to me, very drily, 'I don't think it'll be a problem.'"

With Cohen's approval, Bublé cut the song and it was well received, the *New York Times* praising Michael for transforming it "from a sneak attack into an assertive boast". Nick Cave's version, which appears on the soundtrack to the film *Leonard Cohen: I'm Your Man* is worth a listen, but Michael's bass-driven take, dripping with bravado and sounding like it comes straight out of a James Bond movie, is surely a worthy rival.

Turning the intensity down a few notches, 'Comin' Home Baby' was written by jazz musicians Bob Dorough and Ben Tucker for Mel Tormé's 1962 album of the same name. Michael's version was done as a duet with hit R&B vocal trio Boyz II Men, giving the song a sweet soul feel. Nathan, Shaun and Wanya's signature harmonising drove Michael's lead vocals and added a healthy dose of jazz to the proceedings.

After 'Lost' comes the album's title track. 'Call Me Irresponsible' was written in 1962 by the legendary team of Jimmy Van Heusen and Sammy Cahn and, according to legend, was originally intended for Judy Garland and her then-forthcoming CBS television show. Many years later, lyricist Cahn revealed the song was written for Fred Astaire and the film *Papa's Delicate Condition*. Contractual problems prevented Astaire from making the film, the lead role eventually going to Jackie Gleason. The song proved its pedigree by winning the Academy Award for Best Original Song, and was later successfully covered by Frank Sinatra.

'Wonderful Tonight' was written by Eric Clapton while waiting for his then-wife Patti Boyd to get ready for an evening out. Butch Baker later did a country cover, while UK vocal group Damage's R&B-influenced interpretation made number three in the UK in 1997. To make it distinctively different, Michael framed his version as a duet with Brazilian singer and songwriter Ivan Lins.

A superstar in his native country, Lins' brand of romantic jazz-pop had earned him international respect. His songs had been recorded by many American artists, including Ella Fitzgerald, Sarah Vaughan, Carmen McRae, Nancy Wilson, Patti Austin, Take Six, Lee Ritenour, Dave Grusin and Sergio Mendes. It's likely the tie-up was engineered by David Foster with a view to increasing Michael's profile on the South American continent.

"I've always been very sentimental about that song," Bublé revealed of 'Wonderful Tonight'. "What is interesting about the track is: here I am, a 31-year-old guy from Canada who's singing a song that meant so much to me with a 61-year-old man from Brazil who's singing in his own language, but it means the exact same thing to both of us."

Michael's composition 'Everything' was indicative of his new-found fulfilment and would be his first single. Following the success of 'Home', he again enlisted the talents of Alan Chang and Amy Foster-Gilles. While Michael admitted that new-love Emily Blunt was in his thoughts, his concern was just as much about the fans and how they'd take to the track. It was a clear statement of intent.

"I love pop music, and I was hoping I could do what I do and delve a little closer to acoustic pop without being called schizophrenic," he said. "I wrote a melody with a nice Seventies summer feel, and I sat with a lyricist to write about being newly in love.

"When I was writing it, I did think about Emily, and I would love to say cheesily that I just have one person in mind when I'm writing a song, but there's a formulaic thing that's happening there," he told TheStar.com. "I'm thinking, is this a catchy hook? Have I written a great melody that people are going to go home and sing in the shower? I told Amy I wanted 'Everything' to talk about all of the things that just one person can be to you."

The song ditched the big-band feel of a typical Bublé recording and, instead, went for a straightforward contemporary pop feel. It found moderate success, charting in the UK Top 40 and hitting number 46 in the *Billboard* Hot 100. Maybe it wasn't as successful as Michael would have hoped, but the departure it represented and the versatility it displayed was perhaps more important.

Though he enjoyed writing his own material, Michael conceded that it might never become a full-time gig: "I don't know if I'm ever going to do the all-original thing. I love reinterpreting these great standards. There's a reason why some of these songs are 90 years old and people still know them: they talk about things that are always going to be relevant: love and loneliness and betrayal."

Next up was 'I've Got The World On A String', a song that dates back to 1932 when it was written by Harold Arlen and Ted Koehler for the *Cotton Club Parade*. Over the years it has been recorded by Cab Calloway, Bing Crosby, Frank Sinatra and, most recently, Tony Bennett as a duet with Diana Krall. Michael had again dipped into the Great American Songbook with great success.

'Always On My Mind' is one of the most popular songs of the twentieth century. Written by Johnny Christopher, Mark James and Wayne Carson Thompson and originally recorded in 1972 by Brenda Lee, the most notable of the more than 300 cover versions have been recorded by Willie Nelson, Elvis Presley and the Pet Shop Boys. The Nelson version, released in 1983, won the Grammy Award for Best Male Country Vocal Performance and enabled the composition belatedly to win awards for Song of the Year and Best Country Song.

'That's Life' was the title track to Frank Sinatra's 1966 album and was written by Dean Kay and Kelly Gordon. When released as a single in its own right it made it to number four on the *Billboard Hot 100*. It has since been recorded by artists as diverse as The Temptations, Aretha Franklin, James Brown, David Lee Roth, Bono and Westlife.

The album closes with 'Dream', a 1944 Johnny Mercer song that was later a hit for The Pied Pipers and Frank Sinatra. Before Michael, the definitive recording was probably Ella Fitzgerald's version for her 1964 album *Sings The Johnny Mercer Songbook*.

As with *It's Time*, a stellar cast of musicians had been assembled to appear on the album, including Paulinho Da Costa (percussion), Nathan East (bass), Greg Phillinganes (piano) and Siedah Garrett (vocals). Once again, in producing the best album possible it made sense to use the very best musicians and singers.

The 13-track result was finally ready for release on the first day of May 2007, but it was given something of a pre-release boost when Michael was invited to appear on the *American Idol* series six results show. Ironically, Michael was a late replacement for his friend Tony Bennett and chose to sing his new album's title track 'Call Me Irresponsible'. But what should have been an enjoyable experience did not go exactly as planned.

"I was disappointed with myself for that performance," he admitted, "but I'd done a video for my new single the day before. I was doing a song I've never done before live in front of thirty-five million people, I'm covering for the greatest singer ever and, to be honest, I'm terrified. My mom rang me after and said I looked very nervous but seemed to relax more as it went along."

It says much for Michael's own values that he would be critical of his performance on such a widely seen television programme. It was this constant pursuit of excellence that had taken him to the top of his profession and would enable him to remain there. As it turned out few, if any, of his fans were left disappointed, a tribute to Michael's professionalism.

Indeed, those members of his fan club fortunate enough to be given a sneak preview of the album and video for the single 'Lost' were impressed with the development Michael had shown on this new album. Thanks to the power of the Internet, this further increased the expectation for *Call Me Irresponsible* ahead of release.

The album did not disappoint. Entering the *Billboard* chart at number two, it moved up a place a week later to dislodge rapper Ne-Yo's *Because Of You* to register Michael's first ever US number one album. It had sold 145,000 copies in the second week and took the top spot, seeing off the challenge of Bone Thugs-n-Harmony's *Strength & Loyalty*. The achievement was made all the more special by the realisation that it put Michael in exalted company, for the only other artists ever to have entered the chart so high and then risen to the summit were Mary J Blige, Hilary Duff, Michael Jackson, NWA and Sugarland.

Although *Call Me Irresponsible* spent just one solitary week at the top of the chart, it would go on to sell over two million copies in the States, earning another double-platinum award from the RIAA. The success of the album proved that Michael had anticipated what his audience wanted and what he needed to do, both to keep them happy and to attract new fans along the way.

"I wouldn't be happy singing all originals. It's just not me. Maybe that'll bite me on the butt, but my passion is interpreting the greatest songs ever written. I do feel a duty to the vocalists who've inspired me and to those writers responsible for what's termed the Great American Songbook to help keep this music properly alive, not just ticking over on a respirator. I want it to be in the contemporary mainstream, not some museum piece.

"Not to put down Kelis, but do you think in 80 years people will be paying money to hear someone sing, 'My milkshake brings all the boys to the yard'? I don't think so. It seems the music I fell in love with isn't quite so disposable as a lot of pop music."

The album's cover followed the established pattern of featuring a portrait of the main man. But this one was different. It was taken by veteran photographer Bill Claxton, whose past subjects had included actor Steve McQueen and iconic jazz trumpeter Chet Baker, and whose daily fees approached $50,000. Claxton, a major jazz fan who sadly passed away in 2008, had also helped establish the organisation that runs the Grammy Awards.

The pair had met in strained circumstances when Claxton's ailing cat had wandered onto a Hollywood property Bublé was renting. He took the apparent stray to the nearest vet, who declared it sick and with little hope of recovery. When Claxton's wife found out the ailing feline had been put to sleep, she was less than pleased – but fences were mended when Michael's explanation that he was only being helpful was accepted, and the fence-mending continued with the commission for the album's photography.

While the album proved a runaway smash, the singles taken from it kept interest alive for much of the rest of the year. 'Everything' was released some two weeks after the album and would go on to top the Hot Adult Contemporary Tracks chart. It also made the Top 40 in the UK and was a chart hit six months later when Michael was in the UK.

'Me And Mrs Jones' was seriously considered for release as a single – to the extent that a video was shot for it – but someone had second thoughts shortly before release and the single was shelved (although thiat did not prevent the track hitting the Swiss charts). 'Lost' was released in its place on 1 October and registered on the *Billboard Hot 100*, while subsequent releases 'It Had Better Be Tonight' and 'Comin' Home Baby' also attracted considerable radio play. 'Lost' also became Michael's first Top Twenty hit in the UK, peaking at number 19 during the course of its 15-week chart run.

As impressive as the album's performance was in America, it was the rest of the world that took to it in a big way. In the UK, the album entered the chart at number two and would go on to earn a gold award for sales in excess of 100,000 copies. Five months later a special edition (effectively a two-CD tour edition) of the album, featuring exclusive remixes and additional tracks, proved to be one of the biggest sellers in the country in the run-up to Christmas, peaking at number three on the chart but going on to sell nearly a million copies and to be certified triple platinum. This version would also register more than a year on the chart, appearing on the listings for 56 weeks.

European sales of the special edition would eventually top the two-million mark, earning more awards from the IFPI. In Australia, the album had three separate spells at number one on the charts and sold over 350,000 copies, going platinum five times over. *Call Me Irresponsible* would eventually top the charts in Canada, the US, Portugal, Italy, Australia, Ireland, Germany and Holland and make the Top Ten just about everywhere else. Total worldwide sales to date for *Call Me Irresponsible* are 6.5 million and counting.

It was a fact that evaded all but the most studious of music-business analysts, but, when Michael made it to number one on the US album chart in July 2007, he ended a 13-year record. Although Vancouver noise-merchants Nickelback had managed the feat, as had Celine Dion, Bublé was the first Canadian male solo artist since Bryan Adams to scale the chart.

Adams, whose *Reckless* had topped the pile back in August 1985, was gracious enough to acknowledge the man who had matched him as "a good singer". But it took more than raw talent alone to reach the heights, in Stateside terms at least. A shrewd marketing campaign included appearances on *American Idol* and *Oprah*, two shows that, between them, just about reached anyone of any age with the slightest interest in the music Bublé purveyed.

As already recounted, Bublé had found his own *Idol* appearance unconvincing. "There were probably 80,000 people about to buy the record who went, 'Oh, he's really not that good.' I don't know how much that helped. Maybe it put you in the consciousness of some of the American public."

He did, however, admit that a showcase appearance on Oprah Winfrey's top-rated talk show, a prospect he found rather less daunting, was "good for 35,000 or 40,000 records for that week and the next couple of weeks. That kind of power is pretty amazing. It was quite shocking to me to see that kind of impact."

Just as he had done for the previous albums, Michael travelled the globe in support of the album, appearing on countless television programmes, either being interviewed or actually performing. One such appearance was in autumn 2007 on the top UK television talent show *The X Factor* – the UK equivalent of *American Idol*. Indeed the shows shared a judge in Simon Cowell.

Michael revealed that, early on in his career, he would have contemplated going on one of the many television talent contests as a way of gaining his big break. "I would have gone on *Pop Idol*. I would have done *anything* to make it. I was on the club circuit for ten years and on the verge of giving up." But he didn't, and in retrospect feels the experience of learning his craft as an entertainer was vital. "On shows like that, you take these kids from high school and, all of a sudden, they're stars. I failed for ten years and learned from my mistakes. I really feel for the kids on these shows sometimes because they have such expectations."

One of the contestants in that year's series, the fourth, was Leon Jackson, a young singer from West Lothian. Although Michael's own mainstream breakthrough had only occurred some three years previously, Jackson was quick to name Michael as an inspiration, claiming he was a big fan of contemporary jazz and that Michael was the artist he most aspired to be.

The cynical might say the adoration was stage-managed, since it was already agreed that Michael would appear on the show. True, the extremely large viewing figures the show attracted (the final that year was watched by 12 million viewers) meant it was not a show Bublé would knowingly turn down, especially as he got to sing 'Lost'. However, Michael was impressed enough with Leon and his performances to invite him to join him on stage at Wembley Arena in December to perform a duet of 'Home'.

Michael's 2007 British tour took in nine arenas, kicking off at Brighton Centre on November 23 and passing through Birmingham (24), Cardiff (30) and Nottingham (December 2) before ending at Wembley Arena on the fourth. Top-price tickets were a reasonable £37.50, with Wembley rounding prices up to £40. The *Daily Mail* reviewed the shows by suggesting that the headline act was "A one-man Rat Pack who has lived, loved and brawled, but polishes up well in a sharp suit." His secret, they said, was that there was "something edgy and dangerous about him that contrasts with the comfort zone of his singing". His audience, the *Mail* concluded, consisted of "couples in love and smartly attired youngish ladies".

As success piled upon success, Michael proved he was keeping his feet planted very much on the ground – and that the tantrums and diva-esque behaviour of recent years were very much in the past. "I'm intolerable," he smiled self-mockingly. "I actually hire someone just to feed me prawn-cocktail crisps, one by one. I have to be carried, I don't do stairs any more, and I'm also to be called 'The Maestro' whenever people are around. I like to go home and just burn money, sometimes a hundred dollars at a time."

His well-developed sense of humour got another airing at the Juno Awards held in Calgary on April 6, 2008. Michael had received a total of five nominations, for Artist of the Year, Album of the Year and Pop Album of the Year for *Call Me Irresponsible,* Single of the Year for 'Everything' and Juno Fan Choice Award. In the event he won just one, the Fan Choice Award. On stage, Michael announced, "This is for all those people who said I couldn't vote for myself enough times to win." He later thanked awards sponsor Dorito tortilla chips "for making such tasty treats. Sometimes when I eat them, my fingers, they go orange, but it's worth it!"

He returned to the same theme backstage after the ceremony, when his humour became rather more risqué. "I *do* love Doritos. I just learned when you're eating them, you should never watch dirty movies or anything like that. It's true. I thought there was something really wrong with me, but it was just the Doritos."

There were to be other awards that year, including two nominations and two wins from the Canadian Smooth Jazz Awards for Best Male Vocalist and Best Original Composition for 'Everything'. Michael also got his first nomination from the UK, finding himself up against Bruce Springsteen, Rufus Wainwright, Timbaland and Kanye West in the Brit Awards' International Male Artist category. The trophy was carried home by Kanye West, who, like Michael, had enjoyed an exceptional year in the UK and fully deserved his victory.

But there was more than adequate compensation to come from the Grammy Awards in Los Angeles. Michael was nominated in two categories that year. In Best Male Pop Vocal Performance, his 'Everything' was up against John Mayer and 'Belief', Paul McCartney and 'Dance Tonight', Seal with 'Amazing' and Justin Timberlake's 'What Goes Around Comes Around'. The award would be taken by Timberlake, a popular winner on the night.

The second category was Best Traditional Pop Vocal Album, with Michael being nominated for *Call Me Irresponsible*. After his outburst 12 months previously, he would no doubt have been especially pleased that Tony Bennett had not released an album during the qualifying period! Instead, Michael was competing against Barbra Streisand's *Live In Concert*, Queen Latifah's *Trav'lin' Light*, Bette Midler's *Cool Yule* and James Taylor's *James Taylor At Christmas*. Irrespective of when the award was handed out and how many were tuned in, Michael's ultimate victory over a quartet of musical giants was a career-defining moment for him. "Winning a Grammy is a dream come true. It was a first for me and you always remember your first time. It makes it doubly exciting to get back on the road to perform for my fans."

Those fans were beginning to be drawn from all walks of life and Michael worked hard to ensure everyone left at the end of the evening happy and content. "I get everyone coming to my show – gay, straight, black, white – and they all bop to the same songs. It's a testament to the music."

Gay fans had not been backward in coming forward and attracting Michael's attention. They could prove particularly persistent, too, as the singer found when a fan made an explicit call from the hotel lobby in the middle of the night. "I told him I'd come down and hit him – not because of what he wanted to do to me, but because he was phoning my room at that time of the morning." His biggest fan in the UK, meanwhile, was sometime cross-dressing TV personality Paul O'Grady, who was happy to broadcast his devotion to 'The Bublé', as he called him.

As well as being openly all-inclusive in his appeal, Michael also ensured ticket prices were kept at a reasonable level, something very few artists were concerned with. "I had a promoter overseas tell me every ticket would be AUS$99. I said, 'That's not fair, you can't charge $99 if they're in an arena 70 metres away from you.' I told Paul Dainty I wanted the ticket prices brought down. My dad called me and said, 'Mike, your gross is going to be lower.' I'm not saying I don't like making money out of making music, but it's not about the gross of a tour, it's about showing appreciation to an audience.

"It's about letting the guy making thirty grand a year come with his family. It's not going to kill him to bring his family. He bought my record too, so why should he pay a hundred and fifty dollars for a ticket? If I play theatres, yeah, I get it, it's intimate. But not if I'm an arena act, no way. I'm not so out of touch with reality to not know it's a big deal to come out to a show. If a family comes there's parking, restaurant, babysitters – that all adds up to a lot of money."

The working-class ex-fisherman was clearly not about to forget his own family's struggles to make ends meet. "I've made more money than I ever thought I would. I've sold more albums than I ever thought I would, I want people to know I'm not ripping them off. Some bands charge five hundred dollars a ticket. Who can come to that show? I don't care if Sinatra comes back from the dead, I ain't paying five hundred dollars a ticket. It's nice to build an audience slowly. I still feel like the underdog. Even though maybe I'm not, but I still feel like the underdog."

This concern for the amount of money his audience was paying for a ticket puts Michael in a very small and select band of artists. It also goes some considerable way to explaining why his ever-growing audience has remained faithful from the start. That, and his gradual development as an artist, would seem to be the key to longevity in an industry that only bestows it on a select few.

"I have a real strong feeling that if you keep giving people the same thing, they'll go, 'Honey, I've got four Bublé albums, we don't need another.' I understand the record company needs product and that it's a business, but I'm here for a career. When something comes out, I want it to *last*. I want my record to be on the chart for a year or two. I don't want to come out with something every few months – to me that reeks of insecurity, from the artist and the company.

"I'm not in the record business. This is not about CDs, this is about creating a brand name, putting on a great show so that when the next album comes out, people will be excited to hear what I've done next. I'm stockpiling songs. I'll do whatever works. I was listening to Kenny Rogers the other day. I love Kenny. The duet he does with Sheena Easton, 'We've Got Tonight', is a really great song. Bob Seger wrote it. I listened to that and went, 'Here's a really pretty song'."

So were we about to see the advent of Bublé the 'Hat Act'? Apparently nothing was being ruled out. "Maybe I could do something that's a bit country. Maybe turn ['We've Got Tonight'] into a beautiful, sexy duet that takes things on a different angle. I know people think it's cheesy, but I don't have that problem with Kenny Rogers. His version is beautiful. I was born in 1975. It's not in my memory. I have no connection to it emotionally so, when I hear it, it's just raw."

Irrespective of the genre Michael felt he belonged in, his audience accepted him as one of the best singers currently on the market. The diversity of his repertoire meant he could in turn attract a diverse audience; every age group and gender was represented, as Michael had previously noted. Every date was sold out within hours of tickets going on sale, meaning there were countless thousands around the world who would be disappointed at not getting their hands on the hottest ticket in town. Fortunately, Michael had released a succession of live CDs since he first made his major chart breakthrough, which went some way towards compensating those unable to get a ticket and provided those who did with the perfect memento of his live show.

On December 5, 2008, Michael brought his own special show to Madison Square Garden, his first appearance at the iconic New York venue. In many ways, the selection of venue was pre-ordained, for it was at Madison Square Garden in 1974 that Frank Sinatra had recorded his legendary TV special and album, *The Main Event*. Michael would also make a triumphant return to the Blue Note jazz club while in the city, having previously appeared there in 2002. Both his performances were recorded and filmed for posterity.

In fact, the DVD section of the eventual package – his third such presentation, after *Come Fly With Me* and *Caught In The Act* – was, for the most part, a documentary of Michael's date at the Garden. It featured extensive backstage footage, as well as film of Michael with his family, who all travelled down to see the boy from BC make New York City his own.

Backed by his own big band, the entire package showcased the full experience of a Michael Bublé concert: the almost instant rapport he has with his audience, his at-times wicked sense of humour and, most importantly, the carefully paced show that leaves the audience eager for more.

Michael Bublé Meets Madison Square Garden featured a 10-track CD together with a 60-minute DVD. The package was trailed on Michael's own website ahead of release, and members of his fan club were given the opportunity to buy an exclusive version that contained an extra two audio tracks. The version that was available on general sale was released on June 16, 2009 and made it to number 14 on the *Billboard* Top 200 chart, an extremely impressive return for a live album. It also topped the trade paper's jazz chart and would feature highly in listings around the world, including making number 22 in the UK.

Fan-club members also got an early taste of a song Michael would eventually feature on his next album, the old Dean Martin number 'You're Nobody Till Somebody Loves You', which was featured on the DVD. "That'll be on the next record, I'll produce that myself," said Michael, giving his fans a hint of the next big step forward he had planned for his career. "I'm doing that in New York in September."

But that was still in the future, for there was still the little matter of travelling around the world promoting *Meets Madison Square Garden*. It was a labour of love that would culminate in another nomination for a Grammy Award for Best Traditional Pop Vocal Album. It was his third in the category, following his win in 2008 with *Call Me Irresponsible* and a nomination for *Caught In The Act*.

In 2007 *Caught In The Act* had missed out, as Michael had foreseen, when Tony Bennett collected the award; in 2010 the two artists would again be going head to head, with Tony's album *A Swingin' Christmas,* joining Harry Connick Jr's *Your Songs*, Liza Minnelli's *Liza's At The Palace!* and Willie Nelson's *American Classic* in competition. In fact, it could be said that the competition for the 2010 award was even stronger than in both 2008, when Michael had won, and 2007, when he hadn't.

Perhaps against the odds, Bublé beat Bennett to the punch and carried off his second Grammy Award. Again the presentation was made during the non-televised segment of the show, but this time there was no outburst from Michael.

If anything, Bublé had grown up very quickly by the time *Call Me Irresponsible* and *Meets Madison Square Garden* hit the market. He appreciated his success and he appreciated his audience. "The songs I sing are universally loved and transcend all borders… At my shows I see a group of bikers and then groups of women on a girls' night out and everyone's just singing along. I think that's a testament more to the music than it is to me."

By the time the promotional work and tours for *Call Me Irresponsible* and *Meets Madison Square Garden* had run their course, Michael had performed in some 40 countries around the world, in front of thousands of longstanding fans and recent converts. His total record sales had now surpassed the 20 million mark and were still rising, even as thoughts began to turn to a new album. With such sales came financial rewards, the likes of which Michael could only have dreamed about as he started his long trek to stardom.

His new-found fame and wealth also enabled him to indulge himself and, more importantly to him, his family and friends. "The success is worth nothing to me if I can't share it with the people I love. I think most of us are like that though. I don't think I'm doing something crazy." It was reported that various members of the family had been given Christmas gifts of suitcases containing $1 million in cash and the deeds to various homes. Not that Michael was willing to confirm or deny such rumours of his generosity.

"Maybe those people haven't had the family I've had. The money never mattered. I'm not kidding you. It hasn't really brought me any kind of happiness. Maybe a little more comfort – not having to worry about my future and my family's future. I guess that's a bigger deal than I make it out to be. I don't really have anything really fancy… I have houses and all the shit! But I don't wear fancy jewellery."

There was one artist in particular Michael used to illustrate what he wanted to be. "Look at Neil Diamond. Was he the cool guy? No, he was the housewives' guy. He didn't try to be what he wasn't.

He just did what he did – made great music, was a good entertainer, nice-enough guy. And, boy oh boy, is he hip as shit now! Nice guys do finish first sometimes."

They say you can tell a man by the company he keeps, and by this time Michael Bublé was nothing if not in demand to interact with his fellow artists. Having sung on Tony Bennett's 2006 duets disc, he was the only male vocalist to be invited to contribute to a new Ella Fitzgerald tribute CD. A portion of the proceeds went to the foundation she had established to provide grants in the areas of music education and appreciation, academic enrichment and work with disadvantaged children.

Released in 2007, *We All Love Ella* was recorded to celebrate the 90th anniversary of the late jazz legend's birth. Its other featured artists included Natalie Cole, Chaka Khan, Gladys Knight, Queen Latifah, Etta James, Dianne Reeves, Linda Ronstadt and Lizz Wright. All tackled numbers associated with the First Lady of Song, Michael's choice being 'Too Close For Comfort' – a performance Amazon's website rated "so slick it would put an eel to shame"! In spite of being the only man involved he wouldn't have felt alone, being accompanied by fellow Canadians Diana Krall and kd lang.

The engagement had an amusing side since, when Michael had heard a recording by Ms Fitzgerald and Louis Armstrong as a boy, he had assumed Ella was the male singer, since he had misheard Louis as 'Louise' Armstrong. Happily for his fans, he lived down the embarrassment to sing another day.

As the first decade of the new millennium progressed, Michael Bublé's personal and professional lives were in equally good shape – or so it seemed. His irresponsible years were over, and his standing in the music business was assured. For now, there was real happiness behind that ready smile.

CHAPTER 6

Crazy Love

There comes a time when any protégé yearns to break free from their Svengali's embrace and prove they can stand up for themselves. So often in pop music, however, the artist has fallen flat on their face as it becomes apparent just how instrumental their producer/songwriter/starmaker was in putting together the whole package.

The moment of reckoning appeared to be close for Michael Bublé in 2009 as he contemplated his fourth major-label release. It was certainly the case that, in the best part of the decade that they had been associated, David Foster had paid him assiduous attention. But there had been tensions, most notably the 'Lady In Red' episode. Michael felt a line had been crossed.

In another interview, he gave vent to the increasingly obvious feeling that he was something of a puppet. "Yes, producers and people at the record company are still trying to control what I do, in some instances very heavily. I understand they're just trying to do what they think is right, and I love that they give me advice. I really do. I'm hungry for their wisdom and knowledge. But it's my face on the CD sleeve and me who wins or loses as a result of what I put out. Having listened, watched and learned, I now know exactly who I am and what I want to do."

He hinted heavily that the time had come to take his studio destiny into his own hands and produce his own music. In fact, for someone who had come such a long way in a matter of a few years, he seemed in some respects remarkably dissatisfied with his lot. On the positive side, it was clear he was still striving to build his audience and to develop as an artist, and he still had the hunger to succeed that so many stars lose as their careers blossom – to the detriment of their music.

It wasn't that Michael felt he had yet to make the break into the big time, but rather he was determined to stay there, come what may. Having sold six million copies of his previous album, Bublé was distressed when Warner Bros chairman Tom Whalley told him that global sales for his next release were estimated at a likely two or three million.

The problem, of course, was downloading. With the music industry in crisis, many artists had resigned themselves to selling fewer records. Bublé, however, had other ideas. "But I said, 'No, I'm not the same as other artists, I won't be affected in the same way. I'm telling you Tom, we're going to sell seven or eight million.'"

Bublé's reasoning was that, while downloading made it easy for consumers to cherry-pick individual tracks rather than buy the whole package as the artist conceived it, his albums were quality from first track to last. "Other artists write 13 songs and hopefully one or two of them are successful singles. And the other 11, for the most part, are filler. And I think people have grown tired of spending £15 for the two singles they like, so they download them. Everyone bitches about downloading, but a lot of artists put out shit. And I think part of the reason I'm so fortunate is that I get to cover some of the greatest songs of all time. So there's quality."

The important thing for Bublé as an artist, he said, was "to really passionately believe there were 12 or 13 really good songs. Not a 'skipper'. There's so much to lose now. I'm so excited and so terrified at the same time. I don't want people to hate it. I want them to love it. Every artist's nightmare is to be in the 'Whatever happened to?' file."

Michael was well abreast of the times and was willing to harness the power of the Internet in his favour. He piqued fans' curiosity by releasing snippets of information about his new album online, using social network Facebook and his website's 'official online newspaper', *The Daily Bublé*, in the summer of 2009.

The title was to be *Crazy Love,* named after a track on Van Morrison's LP *Moondance*. Bublé had already, of course, paid homage to the album's title track on his self-titled debut.

The original release date of 13 October was brought forward four days, much to his fans' delight, to coincide with an appearance on the *Oprah Winfrey Show*. Bublé was once again hobnobbing with US TV royalty as anticipation was building for his latest release, and another appearance on this tried-and-tested promotional platform was an ideal way to publicise the album.

Bublé used a slot on another US talk show, *LX New York,* to explain that his new album would be conceptual and would explore the subject of love. When his host suggested, "If it ain't broke don't fix it," Michael replied. "I think you've got to show growth. I think your audience gets bored and they go to the store and the girl goes, 'Honey I want to get the Bublé record', and the guy goes, 'It's 15 bucks, babe – we got three of them already!'

"But this one's different; this one takes you to a new place. It explores the ins and outs of love. Love is a very complicated word, and when you're in love it comes with insecurities and jealousy and passion. I really wanted to sing about the spectrum."

The lower points of love explored on the album would be

fuelled by Michael's recent and well-publicised break-up with Emily Blunt, something he felt helped create a more authentic record. "When you go through something like that, you either let it get you down or you take the opportunity to work on yourself and become a better guy, and I used it to try to become a better person and a better artist. I wish I didn't have to go through what I went through to make this record, but I did and I'm glad I did, because today's curse is tomorrow's blessing and I made a record that I'm really proud of."

The reasons for his split with Emily after some three years will be covered in greater depth in chapter seven. But if Blunt was the inspiration for the darker points on *Crazy Love,* then a new girlfriend, Argentinean actress and model Luisana Lopilato, certainly helped create the lighter parts. She would appear in the video for Michael's first single from the album, 'Haven't Met You Yet', which was also the song he sang to launch the LP on *Oprah.* It was another Bublé original and Michael returned to songwriting partners Alan Chang and Amy Foster-Gillies to help him create it. The song would soon become one of his signature tunes.

The video shows Michael and Luisana meeting and falling in love in the middle of a supermarket. Michael said it was an easy decision to include his actress girlfriend in the video. "To be honest, I didn't want to have to hire an actor. It was far easier for me conceptually to do this with her and to be really comfortable to be able to be a total dork! You can see because the whole video I'm smiling... I'm a complete dumb-ass and I loved every minute!"

UK website *Digital Spy,* reviewing the track, labelled it "a toe-tapping pop tune with lavish production – the strings swell in all the right places, the brass parps perkily and the lyrics are so shamelessly romantic Barry Manilow could sing them." Others discerned a nod to the Beatles in the 'Love love love' refrain, harking back to Michael's earlier Fab Four cover 'Can't Buy Me Love' on *It's Time.*

'Haven't Met You Yet' charted at number 24 in the *Billboard Hot 100*, Michael's highest position to date, and would hit the top spot in the Adult Contemporary charts. The track was even nestled in the Top 40 in *Billboard's* year-end charts and reached number five in the UK, a nation that was fast taking Michael to their hearts.

Crazy Love was emotionally stripped back and Michael wanted that reflected in the simplified recording techniques. "I tried to go back to the old-school way of recording. Two or three of the tracks are done to eight-track, which was a first for me. Then quite a few of the old ones, the standards like 'Stardust', were done live off the floor, mistakes and all."

But it was those mistakes and flaws, he felt, that were part of what makes the music special. He also tried to concentrate on the words and not worry so much about the delivery, "just thinking about being as honest as I can be, and catching a vibe, a moment. When I listened to a take of a song, I wouldn't choose it because I thought my voice sounded nice, I would choose it because I thought I hade conveyed the emotion."

Michael's decisions were also based on his hankering for a bygone era of organic music. "I like hearing the flaws and the pops, I like hearing the changes in tempo. I like hearing the air in the room, there's something cool about that. When I listened to Sinatra he was like a rock god! I know that that sounds weird for people, but it's so raw: his drummer is bashing the shit out of those drums and you can hear the horn section just playing so hard.

"It's not like it is now, where the guitar is done in this room, and the door is closed on the drums, and everything is completely separated and it's sterile. I wanted all the doors to be open; I wanted the mics hung from the ceiling. I didn't know how to do it, so I called Humberto Gatica, who engineered it, and I said 'Can we do this the old-school way so I can feel something?'"

He believed the album also offered a departure from his earlier work, when he had been "marketed as the singer who would appeal to your grandma", and enabled him to appeal to a broader, younger audience. "Some singers start out as young punks and then make a classics album later in their career," he told the *Daily Mail*. "With me, it has been the other way round. I feel as if I've finally started acting my own age. I'm the Benjamin Button of pop."

Crazy Love certainly demonstrated a giant step forward from his Sinatra-styled past. Indeed, album opener 'Cry Me A River' could have been plucked straight from a James Bond film. It is a shame that the album was released a year after the 007 movie *Quantum Of Solace,* or Bublé may well have featured instead of Alicia Keys and Jack White, such was the track's bombastic swagger.

The song is best known for singer-turned-movie star Julie London's slinky, sexy rendition, which hit the charts way back in 1955 and sold a million copies, but a new generation was happy to acquaint itself with the classic delivered from a male perspective – "A bummer tent of rejection and rage," as Bublé's own website less than poetically put it!

Michael re-opens the Great American Songbook again for 'Georgia On My Mind'. The song was written by legendary songwriter Hoagy Carmichael, achieving fame some 30 years after its creation when Georgia native and blues legend Ray Charles helped it to the number one spot in 1960.

The BBC described Michael's rendition as "a gem", adding, "The gentle string opening with a touch of vibraphone, the close-harmony vocals, his seamless phrasing and a mellow clarinet solo ensure that this account has classic status."

Not content with adding his name to a 'who's who' of classic American artists who had recorded Carmichael's songs, including Louis Armstrong, Bing Crosby, the Dorsey Brothers and Duke Ellington, Michael would record another Carmichael classic on the album. This time he teamed up with New York R&B vocal troupe Naturally 7 for 'Stardust', a recording he had promised fans on the *Meets Madison Square Garden* DVD. "I used to listen to this acappella version of 'Stardust' that Frank Sinatra did when I was a kid," he had told them. "It's so simple and dreamy."

The New Yorkers were an unexpected inclusion on a Bublé CD, but such was Michael's versatility that fans had learnt to expect the unexpected. Michael would return the compliment by helping out Naturally 7 on their cover of Dinah Washington's 'Relax Max' on the 2010 album *Vocal Play*.

The sound of 'Stardust' – a song he had first recorded on his 2002 independent release *Dreams* – is a real throwback to the Thirties and, with Naturally 7's harmonies complementing Michael's velvety tones, the song prompted *Tulsa Today* to claim that "at his core, [Michael] is a jazz singer". Jazz is definitely one string in Michael's bow, but *Crazy Love* displays a mastery of too many genres for him to be so easily pigeonholed.

The second of his co-written tracks was a pure, unadulterated ballad. 'Hold On' again involved Amy Foster-Gillies and Alan Chang, but even though it was released as the second single, the trio's second effort did not gain as strong a reaction from critics and fans as 'Haven't Met You Yet'.

When quizzed on UK TV show *Loose Women,* Michael said he didn't want to tell people what the song was about as he wanted them to interpret it themselves. When pushed, however, he reluctantly revealed more. "In my head it was about a couple, a partnership that didn't work out, and everyone thought it would. But even though things got tough they can still be there for each other, not that they're together but there's some kind of potential for friendship and loyalty." Perhaps it was a message to ex-flames Emily and Debbie…

The Van Morrison-penned title track, 'Crazy Love', followed in the footsteps of Buble's previously successful cover, 'Moondance'.

Bublé announces his appointment as Winter Olympics ambassador in 2009. (RYAN PIERSE/GETTY IMAGES)

Michael Bublé performs on the stage of Desmet studio in Amsterdam on October 30, 2009. (OLAF KRAAK/AFP/GETTY IMAGES)

Honoured to be here? Michael makes his point at the 2010 American Music Awards. (MICHAEL CAULFIELD/AMA2010/GETTY IMAGES FOR DCP)

Bublé at the Beeb! He graces the stage of the BBC Theatre, London, 2009. (MARCO SECCHI/GETTY IMAGES)

Ever-attentive to his fans at New York's Rockefeller Plaza.
(NANCY KASZERMAN/ZUMA/CORBIS)

Home-boy Bublé carries the flame to the Vancouver Winter Olympics, 2010.
(GEORGE PIMENTEL/WIREIMAGE)

Promoting his album *Call Me Irresponsible* at Rose Garden arena in Portland, Oregon. (CORBIS)

Backstage with Welsh singer Katherine Jenkins at the Royal Variety Performance, Blackpool, 2009. (LEON NEAL/ WPA POOL /GETTY IMAGES)

Smile, please! A fan gets the thrill of a lifetime during a concert in Brisbane, 2011. (MARC GRIMWADE/WIREIMAGE)

More smiles as Bublé and bride-to-be Luisana Lopilato hit the 2010 American Music Awards in Los Angeles.
(MICHAEL BUCKNER/AMA2010/GETTY IMAGES FOR DCP)

Merry Christmas Michael! Rocking Z100's Jingle Ball at New York's Madison Square Garden, 2010. (THEO WARGO/WIREIMAGE FOR CLEAR CHANNEL)

Michael, to whom the Irishman was nothing less than an idol, wanted the world to know that he didn't attempt Morrison's songs in a bid to better them, but that his version was going to be "different – my interpretation of the song", and one that, he insisted, "can only come from my life experience and... the love or the loss I've gone through."

'Baby (You've Got What It Takes)', a hit duet for Dinah Washington and Brook Benton in 1960, proved a popular track with fans and critics alike, not least for Michael's recruitment of rhythm-and-blues (in the Fifties sense) revival ensemble Sharon Jones and the Dap Kings. The song was recorded at what Bublé's website called "a tiny little studio hidden away in the noir bowels of Brooklyn" on a "stone-age eight-track device". Once again, Bublé was finding fresh creative challenges for himself. "It was completely outside of what I've ever done – out of my comfort zone, but I had a blast," he said, while The *LA Times* praised Jones for "coaxing Bublé's Sinatra-esque pipes into a soulful purr". Trade paper *Billboard* simply described it as a "slinky R&B romp".

It had become the norm for one track on a Bublé album to step out with a different production style, and on 'Crazy Love', this was it. It was one of five tracks produced by Bob Rock, with whom Michael was enjoying an increasingly fruitful relationship. But Michael would continue his liaison with Sharon Jones when, as the musical guest on *Saturday Night Live* in January 2010, he reprised their song, along with the album's first single, 'Haven't Met You Yet'.

'All Of Me' was a somewhat conservative choice, the jazz standard being one of the most recorded songs of the Thirties. (It had also inspired a movie starring Steve Martin and Lily Tomlin, as well as being massacred by the Muppets!) 'All I Do Is Dream Of You' was a mid-paced plodder in a similar vein, having attracted the attention of artists as diverse as Perry Como, Dean Martin, Judy Garland and even Chico Marx since it took its bow in the 1934 movie *Sadie McKee*.

'You're Nobody Till Somebody Loves You' is a popular song written by Russ Morgan, Larry Stock and James Cavanaugh and published in 1944. Dean Martin recorded it for Reprise Records in 1965, when it reached number 24 on the US pop chart and number one on the easy listening chart, although it had also been covered by Bublé family favourites the Mills Brothers.

Given his comments about recording country material in the vein of Kenny Rogers' version of 'We've Got Tonight', Michael's choice of 'Heartache Tonight' and 'At This Moment' may not have been too surprising. But they were relatively contemporary songs, stemming from the catalogues of The Eagles and Billy Vera respectively. Both had been hit singles in their time, indeed US chart toppers in 1979 and 1987 respectively.

While 'Heartache Tonight' had been The Eagles' fifth number one, 'At This Moment' was Vera's one and only moment at the top, and the song had a story behind it. Originally released in 1981, it was adopted by the later NBC sitcom *Family Ties* during its 1985–86 season as the love theme for the romance between Alex P Keaton (played by Michael J Fox) and his girlfriend Ellen Reed (Tracy Pollan). This prompted Rhino Records to purchase the rights and reissue the song, at which point it topped the *Billboard* chart. To complete the fairy story, Fox eventually married his co-star in real life.

A bonus track was added to the album in the form of 'Whatever It Takes', a song by fellow Canadian Ron Sexsmith. The singer-songwriter had in fact been sending Bublé songs for years in the hope that he might record one. "I never heard back from him," Sexsmith recalls, "and all of a sudden he called me one night to tell me he was going to do this one, which was sort of an odd choice because when I was writing it I was thinking of Bill Withers! I wasn't thinking of Michel Bublé necessarily, but he did a really nice job, he did a sort of Latin version of it."

Interestingly, the song debuted on Sexsmith's 2004 album *Retriever*, released as Michael began his own recording career. Sexsmith might have been surprised by the style in which it was performed, but he was definitely taken aback by the royalties. "Apparently ten million people bought it or something, which is unheard of these days, isn't it?" As he said, "I'm a 35-year-old guy from Canada and I don't write groove oriented-music. So, I can't expect too much." But his lottery number certainly came up when Michael called him.

Meanwhile, another bonus track was added to the UK and European releases of the album in the form of the Bob Rock-produced 'Some Kind Of Wonderful', which had proved a live favourite. The Carole King-penned song was best known from a 1968 recording by Marvin Gaye, itself a revival of the Drifters' 1961 original. But it was time for a new interpretation, and Bublé was happy to provide it.

Critics were, as ever, divided upon the album's release. *The Phili Star* lauded the record and described it as "his best" vocally. However, while the paper claimed Bublé had nothing to prove, it suggested that the "best way to enjoy *Crazy Love* is to take every cut for itself and not as part of a whole. That way, one can really appreciate how Bublé is trying out new stuff, but never without sacrificing the classic melodies and the elegant style he has perfected." A measured review, if not slightly disappointing for an album that Michael considered a concept LP.

The BBC news website said that Michael's decision to leave the musical imperfections in paid off. "Each song thrills the ear as though it were a live performance," it said. *Tulsa Today,* meanwhile, praised his song selection, claiming that the album showed "just how dynamic and versatile the Grammy-winning Canadian is when it comes to picking material".

Crazy Love debuted at number one in the US, selling 132,000 copies in its first week. It would be Michael's second consecutive *Billboard* chart-topping album and an incredible sales feat, given that his competitors that week had enjoyed a three-day headstart following the decision to alter the album's release date to coincide with his appearance on *Oprah*. Despite the apparent handicap, *Crazy Love* clawed back the advantage.

On top of *Crazy Love*'s rapid rise to the top in the States, it also hit number one in the UK, selling more than two million units and going eight-times platinum. The LP would go on to reach number one in six different countries, including Australia, Ireland, Italy and Canada, and achieved multi-platinum status in each one. It also received the re-release treatment just over a year later with a 'Hollywood Edition' complete with bonus tracks, by which time it had racked up sales of more than six million copies worldwide.

This success would not go unnoticed by his peers, and Bublé would receive another Grammy for Best Traditional Pop Vocal Album in 2011. *Crazy Love* would also pick up two Juno awards in Michael's home country for Album of the Year and Pop Album of the Year.

Michael reflected on the album. "I think I was going out of my way to make the least commercial record that I've made. Every artist always says that their next record is the best they've ever made. The first album I was [just] signed and it was a soft record, with tracks like 'How Can You Mend A Broken Heart' and 'Put Your Head On My Shoulder'. I knew that it would be sold to an older generation. But as each record has come, I've enjoyed more power and have become more myself. And each record becomes a bigger statement about who I really am.

"So I thought 'OK kid, you've sold 22 million records, you've done what you had to do, and you were very marketable and commercial. Now you owe it to yourself to make a record for you, that you can listen to, that you really dig,' and I did that."

The production details for the album feature seven credits for David Foster and five for Bob Rock. But Michael and Alan Chang were also given name-checks alongside Humberto Gatica on 'You're

Nobody Till Somebody Loves You', proof perhaps of the singer's continuing growth and evolution. He had not taken the production reins yet, as had been heavily hinted, but if the 'divide and conquer' strategy continued, there seemed a strong possibility that moment was not too far away.

In many ways, Michael Bublé's career path had been the polar opposite of the instant fame offered by *The X Factor*. But he was shrewd enough to see what exposure on the programme could do for his UK profile. So it was that 2009 found him guesting in series six of the show. Bublé was the celebrity mentor for the finalists in week three and also appeared in the series finale, duetting on past single 'Feeling Good' with an unlikely partner.

Essex girl Stacey Solomon was as gauche and unschooled as the Canadian was smooth and sophisticated, but that didn't stop them belting it out. And the besuited Bublé saw his *Crazy Love* album fly off the shelves the following day. Tesco's music buyer Michael Mulligan commented, "*The X Factor* effect shows how popular it is with our customers."

Bublé himself found it "refreshing to see these kids: they are very sweet, they're humble, they want it really bad". But, remembering how close he came to trading his microphone for a pen, he cautioned, "I gotta hope that, at the end of the day, whether they win this thing or not, that doesn't mean it's the be-all and end-all of their careers."

Fellow mentor and former Westlife manager, Irishman Louis Walsh, was suitably impressed. "You have to have the goods to be able to sell it, and Bublé certainly has the goods. I've seen how hard he works, he works the room incredibly well, that's why he's so successful. He's for mummy, daddy, your brother and your sister – *everybody* can like Michael Bublé. But he works hard, he didn't just get there overnight."

Bublé had a strange on-stage doppelganger in the shape of another Irishman, the besuited Dermot O'Leary. The pair got on well and

Buble became a regular guest on O'Leary's BBC Radio 2 shows. (As a result he would be invited in February 2011 to narrate an edition of the radio station's *Song Stories* series. The featured song was Sinatra's classic, 'My Way'.)

O'Leary was also present when, in May 2010, Michael was accorded the compliment of hosting a British TV institution. The *An Audience With…* format had always been restricted to the most mega of stars, and past hosts had included the likes of Dame Shirley Bassey, Lulu, Bruce Forsyth and Elton John. Buble's association with the show was, therefore, recognition that at 34 he had made it.

Of course, it was the kind of show where the audience is almost as much in the spotlight as the featured artist – and looks every inch the part. "I hope at my funeral everyone looks this good!" said Michael as he prepared to face a barrage of pre-scripted questions.

Unfortunately he was clearly a little too at-home with friends and fans such as O'Leary, presenter Holly Willoughby and that year's winner of *The X Factor,* Joe McElderry, in the audience alongside boy-band McFly, actresses Imelda Staunton and Keeley Hawes, longtime fan Paul O'Grady, and another TV talent-show winner, Lemar, who had won BBC's *Fame Academy* in 2002. According to reports in the UK media, when Willoughby asked Michael if he went into the music business in a bid to meet women, he replied, "At 12 years old, I'd have had sex with sandwich meat if it was possible."

The comments were cut, it was said, because bosses were unsure how well their tone would be received by viewers. Michael, however, was relaxed about the whole episode, saying, "I can't see the problem – I see titties after nine o'clock on television here." Whatever the disagreement about his words, what was clear to everyone was Buble's mastery of the musical arts as he served up a selection of hits, including 'Me And Mrs Jones', 'Everything', 'Cry Me A River' and 'Haven't Met You Yet'.

And Michael certainly understood the significance of the show, and its history, even as he joked about it. "It's a huge honour for me to be part of this show, *An Audience With...*, which is a thrill, even though the title is weird for me because 'an audience with Michael Bublé' sounds like I should be wearing a crown and a cape or something – and that's something I only do in my own personal time!"

By the time he closed the show with 'How Sweet It Is (To Be Loved By You)', he had the entire studio on its feet and moving. If a picture was worth a thousand words, then the same could be said for his music. Hopping on one foot, juggling his microphone from hand to hand, this was the charismatic Canadian in his element.

The 12-piece band, each member behind a monogrammed MB stand, hung on his vocal cues and delivered the perfect performance, coached as ever by Alan Chang. It was their solid backing that gave Michael the ease of movement and confidence to strut his stuff – and strut he certainly did! The elongated shape of the platform he performed on, designed to provide maximum stageside seating, offered him some risqué amusement. "Tonight is the first time I can tell you I've been on a phallic stage like this one! I feel like I'm deeply penetrating my audience right now!"

Bublémania had set in just in time for Christmas. And Michael cleverly tied the media furore in with an easy-listening radio station, Magic 105.4, which invited listeners to 'an intimate gig' on December 8, 2009. It would be his only show before the next tour, scheduled for May 2010 and already a sellout. The concert would be held at Air Studios, founded by Beatles producer George Martin and situated in Hampstead, north London.

BBC Radio 2 was still Michael's target market, but its attempt to win over a younger audience who were turned off by Radio 1's diet of rap and R&B meant that, even there, he was now becoming a specialist taste. His mentor, Sir Michael Parkinson, had hung up his headphones in November 2007, and while Michael's pal Jamie

Cullum was being granted the chance to present specialist shows on jazz, the indication was that the station was less and less interested in Michael's kind of music. Not everyone agreed with the station's direction. "It should be the natural home of this music," Parkinson proclaimed in a parting shot to the network, insisting that "there's a market out there that feels starved of it."

So Magic was the choice for this year's promotional blitz – and it responded with full-page ads running across seven newspaper titles, including the *Daily Mail*, *The Times* and the London *Evening Standard*. The response was phenomenal. Tickets for the Air Studios show were snapped up by lucky listeners, while a selection of VIP 'meet-and-greet' tickets were auctioned to raise funds for charity.

Magic 105.4 managing director Steve Parkinson said, "Magic 105.4 has developed an enviable reputation for staging a range of exclusive and intimate gigs with some of the world's top recording artists in unique locations all over London. Michael's concert is a great way for us to celebrate the Christmas holiday and thank our listeners for making Magic 105.4 London's number-one commercial station for almost three years."

Programming director Pete Simmons said, "Whenever we play Michael Bublé songs on Magic 105.4, the station comes alive because he is one of our listeners' favourites. Having him play exclusively for them will be the highlight of the festive season."

Indeed, such was the demand for Michael's talents that he was booked in for a second arena tour, to start in Sheffield in late September 2010 and take in further venues in Newcastle, Nottingham, London, Manchester and Birmingham.

For his part, Michael felt that a special connection had been forged between him and his UK fans in the previous couple of years. 'When I come onto the stage I feel like I've really been accepted, like people have taken ownership of me, and I feel the same way," he said. "They're my family, like I miss them."

He spotlighted the similarities between being a Canadian and a Brit in a very basic way. "We're not American; there's a very different way of life, humour and the way we go about things. I can't explain that; it's just not the same as anywhere else, there's a real connectivity."

He had made a particular connection with English comedian Peter Kay, who admitted that the first time he saw Bublé at the Blackpool Opera House was on the insistence of his grandmother. "I had filmed all day, and it was raining, and my nan said, 'Will you take me?' I thought, 'Oh Christ, I don't want to see this, I just, you know...' but I took her. I picked her up, we went, and it was absolutely amazing. I couldn't tell [enough people about it], I was like, 'You've got to go, you've got to go, you've got to go and see this person. He is incredible.' And I'm not just saying that."

Michael had not known the northern comic, who made the hit video for the 2005 charity re-release of Brit crooner Tony Christie's 'Is This The Way To Amarillo?', until he broke his own unwritten rule and gave him a 'shout-out' during his performance. "I was backstage before the show, and my promoter, said to me, 'Maybe you'd like to say something, there's a comedian in the audience, he's very famous.' And I said, 'I don't do that, I don't do shout-outs. And they said, 'No, but really, he's a great comedian.' And I said, 'Fine, fine.'

"I think the line I said was, 'You know, I guess I'm not supposed to be very funny tonight. Apparently we have one of the country's greatest comedians in the audience. Ladies and gentlemen, Mr Peter Kay', not knowing [who he was]. The audience went so crazy that I remember I was sitting with my mic at the front of the stage, and they didn't stop for so long that I put my mic in my stand and I went back and I sat with my musicians, and I just went, 'What the fuck is going on here?'"

The Canadian then became a fan of Kay's *Phoenix Nights* TV show, watching the DVDs on his tour bus, and the pair struck up an unlikely friendship, to the extent that they discussed their abilities to work an audience and the need to give them a good time. "Me and Peter both talked about the responsibility we have, not only to ourselves but really to this audience who paid good money and have made a big night of it."

Michael admired his new friend because, "while he has a hugely successful career, he sells out arenas, he has hit television shows and makes hit records... at the same time can still walk down the street like a regular guy." There was only one factor marring their friendship. "I just hope he talks slow, because sometimes I can't understand the accent!"

While in Britain, Michael also returned to *The X Factor* arena in October 2010 to promote his new single, 'Hollywood'. He could have been excused for pulling out of his performance as he had been feeling unwell, but he loyally insisted on maintaining his link with the show. Ever the professional, he also took the precaution of lowering the key of the song, as he had doubts he could hit the highest notes. But the storm of criticism he received must have made him think he would have been better off staying in bed.

The controversy arose when he appeared to remove the microphone from his mouth with little or no change on the volume of the vocal that was heard out front. The accusation that he was miming to a pre-recorded backing track hurt him deeply, especially as, he told BBC Radio 1 DJ Scott Mills, "I was flat and out of breath." Explaining his decision to change key, he concluded by asking, "If I was going to lip-synch, wouldn't I just do it to my recording?"

The controversy was further exaggerated by the fact that *The X Factor* judge, Cheryl Cole, had flagrantly mimed her new single in a performance on the same show. That was not Bublé's way. Miming, he insisted, is something he would never do on a television show. "Absolutely not. I never have, never in my life," he said. "I have mimed for videos, but never have I mimed for a live TV show." Michael had simply been practising proper mic technique, but he generously put the criticisms down to the fact that audiences are "too used to seeing people jam mics in their faces because they're lip-synching". He was also willing to offer Cole a getout: "I think if you're dancing [miming is] acceptable."

Such arguments aside, the 2010 tour went as well as had been hoped for. Michael even tested the water regarding his popularity in the UK by venturing out without an entourage in several of the cities they visited. Between two sell-out gigs at the Manchester Evening News Arena, he could not resist popping out for a curry in the city at the East Z East restaurant, followed by a movie at the Printworks. His cover, however, was eventually blown. "East Z East was really good, there was no reaction at all. My friend said, 'It seems like you can get around OK', but then when we walked out of the cinema there was a crowd waiting."

December was a landmark month in the Bublé camp, with two further Grammy nominations falling onto his welcome mat. Michael was up for awards in the category of Best Male Pop Vocal Performance for 'Haven't Met You Yet' and Best Traditional Pop Vocal Album for *Crazy Love*. He added this to his first American Music Award for Adult Contemporary Music – Favourite Artist, decided by a fan vote the previous month.

But there were still performances to be considered, one of which was an invitation to Z100's Jingle Ball Concert at Madison Square Garden in New York City on December 10, an event that included performances by Katy Perry, Justin Bieber, Selena Gomez and Enrique Iglesias. New York's self-styled 'Hit Music Station' only invited the biggest names, and given Michael's affinity with the season this was something of a mark on the popularity barometer.

Meanwhile his *Crazy Love* Tour continued to criss-cross the States, taking in dates in Nashville, Tennessee and Little Rock, Arkansas. By the time Bublé hit the Wells Fargo Center in Philadelphia in late November, he had critics like Amy Sciarretto, reviewing for the Artist Direct website, eating out of his hand. "Swoon. That is what 90 per cent of the crowd does when crooner (and comedian) Michael Bublé saunters across the stage. He's as likeable as they come and boasts oodles of talent, to boot. Can you say total package?

"Indeed, Mr Michael Bublé, who hails from Vancouver, Canada, is a consummate performer, a sharp-dressed man, a crooner who would make the Rat Pack proud. Dean Martin? Frank Sinatra? They'd all open their arms and nod their head with approval for Bublé. That's how damn good he is. Harry Connick, Jr's throne has been usurped by Bublé and there is nothing he can do about it except watch it go."

Sciarretto concluded that "He is husband material: good-looking, smart, witty, charming, classy and well-dressed. He is no label-created pop star. He is as real as it gets."

As if to prove that he hadn't forgotten his fan base across the Atlantic, Bublé invaded millions of living rooms (and undoubtedly stimulated pre-Christmas sales) by means of *This Is Michael Bublé*, an on-the-road documentary of his last British tour. It presented some choice behind-the-scenes moments, as well as giving a taste of our man on stage and in his element.

A number of scenarios were engineered to make the DVD more entertaining, including playing table tennis backstage with the British champions and, a subject always close to his heart, going on the ice with the Nottingham Panthers ice hockey team. Indeed, Bublé requires "one local team hockey puck" in his dressing room as part of his rider contract for concert promoters in every city he performs in, and since December 2008 he has been co-owner of the Vancouver Giants.

At the end of 2010, Michael was also one of the celebrities invited to submit a playlist of his favourite music to iTunes. His selection included some interesting choices. He harked back to Elvis Presley, the man he once imitated in *Red Rock Diner*, for 'Don't Be Cruel', while Leon Russell's original version of 'A Song For You', which had appeared on *It's Time* and by now was Michael's regular set closer, was a tip of the hat to a man who was back in the public eye after many years' absence thanks to *The Union*, a new album recorded with Elton John.

While all-time giants Phil Collins, Willie Nelson and Van Morrison were name-checked, American singer-songwriter Jason Mraz and his song 'I'm Yours' represented the younger generation. Even rap got a look-in in the shape of Kanye West and Jamie Foxx's 'Gold Digger'.

Two further choices reflected Michael's growing interest in South American music, inspired by his new Argentinean love Luisana. The combination of Fifties star couple Keely Smith and Louis Prima's 'Angelina'/'Zooma Zooma' and Mexican singer Julieta Venegas' far more recent 'Limon y Sal' suggested there might be more of a Latin edge to Buble's future output.

The 21st Winter Olympics were hosted by Vancouver that year, and it was always on the cards that the city's favourite singing son would play a part in proceedings. The Olympic torch arrived in the city before the games kicked off on February 12, and Michael was involved in the relay alongside such fellow celebrities as Shania Twain, Arnold Schwarzenegger and, to his delight, hockey legend Wayne Gretzky. Perhaps such serendipity helped bring good luck, for the competition saw Canada win its first competitive gold medal on home soil, having failed to do so on previous occasions when hosting the event in 1976 and 1988.

On the day of the opening ceremony, Michael performed on the NBC channel's *Today* programme, and the BBC selected his rendition of 'Cry Me A River' as the theme for its television coverage. Australian TV also took the opportunity to commission and screen a documentary, *Michael Bublé's Canada*, prior to the Games, with Michael himself co-hosting. It wasn't the first time

Australian television had reflected his popularity down under: the release of *It's Time* in 2005 had been commemorated by a documentary hosted by Ian 'Molly' Meldrum, the antipodean pop critic of choice.

As the Games ended and Canada celebrated its 14 gold medals – a record for a host country – Michael was again present at the closing ceremony, in which the torch was passed on to Sochi in Russia, which would host the next Winter Olympics. His appearance singing 'The Maple Leaf Forever' was memorable, not least for the fact that he was dressed as a Canadian mounted policeman – or Mountie – but then had his uniform removed to reveal a white tuxedo worn underneath.

The 2010 Juno Awards in April were to prove particularly profitable for Michael, as he scooped the Juno Fan Choice Award, Single of the Year for 'Haven't Met You Yet', and Album of the Year and Pop Album of the Year for *Crazy Love*. He was also nominated for, but did not win, Artist of the Year and Songwriter of the Year, both of which went to multi-talented Somali-Canadian singer, rapper and poet K'naan.

Crazy Love producers David Foster and Bob Rock both received separate nominations for Producer of the Year, with Rock emerging victorious. He had also worked with DOA, 311 and The Tragically Hip and, interestingly, would go on to work with Ron Sexsmith, who had contributed 'Whatever It Takes' to *Crazy Love*.

The year ended with a special edition of *Crazy Love,* named the 'Hollywood Edition', which was released on October 18, 2010 in Europe, and a week later in the US. It contained three new studio recordings, including the aforementioned single, 'Hollywood', co-written by Bublé and Toronto-based songwriter Robert G Scott, who had played in Michael's band between 2001 and 2004, and who also played piano and sang backup on the recording. Produced by Bob Rock, the song suggested Michael was still challenging himself and planning new creative collaborations away from his tried-and-trusted team of Chang and Foster-Gillies.

"That's one of the catchiest songs I've ever been part of," said Bublé, adding, "It's kind of like our take on the culture of celebrity and how fucked up it is and how people lose their way in the hunt for fame… It's just one of those things, saying, 'If you're gonna go for it, don't give everything up for it. Remember where you came from… You need to remember what you asked for when you get it'." He also praised Scott as "one of the most dynamic players I have ever had the opportunity to work with. He is simply a force of nature."

Another new song was 'End Of May', a spare, sorrowful ballad by a Seattle-based band called The Actual Tigers about a failed romance. It had been written in 1996 by singer-guitarist Tim Seely and released on the band's 2001 album *Gravelled & Green*; it owed something in style to the US singer-songwriter school of Bob Dylan and Paul Simon. Seely had had a difficult decade, suffering a heart attack in 2009 at age 32, but his fortunes turned around when Alan Chang, a former associate, put the song up to his boss for consideration.

Bublé described the song as "so beautiful I can't even tell you", and was extremely proud of what he brought to it. "I think it might be one of the best vocal performances I've ever given," he said. He was so pleased with the result that he doubted the decision to exclude it from the original release had been the right one. "If I could go back I probably would have replaced something [on the album] with this song… Leaving it off the original release was one of the toughest decisions I had to make… and I'm still not sure I made the right decision."

'Best Of Me' was another new song that, in effect, wasn't so new. It was a mid-Eighties number written by David Foster and originally performed by Foster himself with Olivia Newton-John. Michael had previously reserved the song for live performances, but would only perform it if his mood – and the response of the crowd – was right.

The room had to be silent for Michael to feel he could do the song justice, and if he felt he could not "get there" emotionally it came off the set list.

The 'Hollywood Edition' of *Crazy Love* also included a bonus disc featuring five live versions of Bublé favourites old and new, together with the original versions; this was made available separately in the States via iTunes in the form of an EP, entitled *Hollywood: The Deluxe EP*. A further edition, including a bonus remix CD, making-of DVD and 32-page photo album, was available only through Bublé's official online store.

While some of Michael's fans would be content to be tided over by this 'special edition' while his next studio creation was planned, he would have to live with the fact that expectations were now at fever pitch. All concerned would be hoping that, to quote a past triumph, 'The Best Is Yet To Come'. One burning question, however, remained – who would be pulling the strings?

CHAPTER 7

Away From The Spotlight

Michael Bublé is a ladies' man, of that there is no doubt. But his personal life away from the stage has often made as many headlines as his music.

Nobody was really too bothered in his early days, when he admitted to playing the field with girl fans, but as he has rapidly ascended the showbusiness ladder, some of the tales of his wild life on the road have caused consternation at both his record company and his management, who feel that such stories might damage his clean-cut, heart-throb image.

Bublé himself has made light of this in recent interviews. "My only rule now," he said in 2010, indicating his tour bus, "is that I don't do bus parties. No girls allowed on the bus. In the early days I would have big bus parties and stuff, but no more, it leads to trouble. And you know, I'm about to get married, so, no more bus parties!"

Indeed, as of April 2011 Michael Bublé was a married man. Judging by the response on various online fan forums, his fans have taken to this change of status remarkably well. Not for Michael the John Lennon approach of marrying in secret for fear that his adoring female following might drop him like a stone once he was 'off the market'. Quite the reverse was true: most wished him and his wife Luisana well.

But looking back to the beginning of his career, Michael would cheerfully admit he was no different to most fame-hungry males, attracted by the possibility of female adulation and its potential for physical high jinks. Expanding without inhibition on the theme in 2007 during an interview with the *Daily Telegraph*, he said, "Listen, I would love to tell you that I was this wonderfully smart and full-of-integrity kinda guy. But at the same time, man, I wanted to get *laid*. That was a big part of it! This is why I wanted to be different and why I wanted to have power and fame and money: because I wanted to be attractive to the opposite sex. I'd be lying to you if I didn't say that was a big part of it."

With characteristic humour, Michael told much the same story when interviewed by *60 Minutes* on Australian television two years later, claiming that sex, or the prospect of it, was his main inspiration. "What else is there to think about at 12 or 13? Yeah, I just wanted to get laid, that's really the truth." He went on to confirm, with a smile, that he had succeeded in his ambition.

An incident at his school when he was 15 years old confirmed these pubescent fantasies. "I was rocking by a locker and there was a young girl that I really thought was hot and she had her locker open and there was a photo of Harry Connick Jr in the locker with lipstick kisses all over it. I thought, 'Oh my God, *that* is what I want to be. I want to be the poster with the lipstick kisses in her locker'."

Not that the teenage Michael Bublé was anything like the babe magnet who stares in sultry fashion from the album sleeves of today. Any resemblance to the smooth, suave Harry Connick on the locker door started and ended at the word 'male'. Connick was a world away from the Canadian youth in acid-wash jeans and high-top white trainers with a mullet and hooped earrings.

But Michael's sartorial outlook changed over time, as did his attitude towards the fairer sex. The first major love of his life was Debbie Timuss, an actress, singer and dancer who was also struggling her way up show business' greasy pole. The pair recognised themselves as kindred spirits and understood the value of mutual support in an industry that is likely to suck you in, chew you up and spit you out without compunction.

As has already been recounted, the pair met around 1996 in the cast of the musical *Red Rock Diner* and continued their professional partnership in Dean Regan's big-band revue, *Forever Swing*, in 1998. At that point it was by no means certain who was the brighter prospect. Indeed, while a reviewer of the latter credits Bublé's stage presence, they went on to say, "it's the image of Debbie Timuss' smile and long, lithe legs that seem to capture the spirit of *Swing*."

It seems she captivated more than just the reviewer. In a January 2005 interview with *The Sun*, Bublé confessed, "Seven years ago I met my girlfriend, Debbie Timuss, who was engaged to another man. I stole her off him and fell in love…"

The woman he wooed and won away from the unnamed rival was someone with a down-to-earth view of the entertainment business. "She thinks the whole music thing is a crock of shit, which I like," Michael would smilingly remark.

Debbie's career resumé in the years before she met Michael had included the role of Nancy in the 1995 TV movie *Bye Bye Birdie* starring Jason Alexander, a show called *Dames At Sea* in which she was a dancer, a movie called *Swinging Nutcracker,* broadcast on the Bravo TV channel, and a role in a revival of Tim Rice and Andrew Lloyd-Webber's stage musical *Joseph And The Amazing Technicolor Dreamcoat.*

But if she had come into the relationship as the senior partner in terms of show-business experience, Debbie was soon to find herself left behind as Michael's musical journey took off. The young British

Columbian, who had never left Canada and who found living on the country's east coast exotic, was soon queuing up for his first passport. (An astounded passport official photocopied his driving licence and got him to autograph the copy for his wife!) Foreign travel would soon become second nature to him but, perhaps inevitably, Debbie Timuss was not to make the voyage.

The pair had briefly been engaged, but what should have been one of the most important moments in a woman's life was reduced to farce when, on Valentine's Day 2004, Michael had the ring couriered from Los Angeles to New York and it went missing from the package. Somehow, the consolation prize of a pair of earrings must have seemed symbolic of a lifestyle that left increasingly little time for a relationship.

At first Michael had been faithful, and even expressed how much he missed his girl in song – Debbie was the inspiration for Buble's first original hit single, 'Home'. She had even added backing vocals and appeared in the video. But though his relationship with Timuss ended in late 2005, he still had to perform the song – and relive the relationship – every night on stage.

"At first it was weird," he said. "It was really tough and emotional. It's a very autobiographical song. It was art imitating life imitating art." At times it looked like he was almost going through the motions performing the song. "That can happen," Buble admitted. "You can protect yourself. We'd had a long relationship and it had just ended. But I'm glad I got through it."

Michael's former lover also inspired another song on his third album, *Call Me Irresponsible*. Entitled 'Lost', and penned with the help of a fellow Canadian, songwriter, Jann Arden, it was, Michael said, "an anthem for love that didn't work out. A song for relationships that end, but where you don't want to discard this person you obviously still care for. Just because you're not together doesn't mean you won't love them forever."

Bublé took the trouble to play the song to Debbie before it was released. "She bawled her eyes out," he said. "It was a tribute to us. It would be really callous of me to pretend this history didn't happen." As for Debbie, she went on to make an appearance in 2007's *Fantastic Four: Rise Of The Silver Surfer* movie, but has otherwise kept a low profile while her former fiancé continued his ascent to global stardom.

So why did they split? The usual story of growing apart appeared to be a large part of the reason. "I was working, she was working. It got to be that we were never together and so we grew apart. Facing up to that was pretty crushing for both of us."

But Michael also admitted his head was turned by the prospect of cashing in sexually on his fame. "I had this success and I thought people needed to think I was single for my image. We split because I just started ignoring her and sleeping around. I was immature."

This was a breathtakingly frank admission, the like of which few entertainers would dare come out with. And there was more. "After struggling 10 years in obscurity, all of a sudden fame and fortune came and I got a little bit ahead of myself. I was rude and reckless with girls, and I just thought, 'Fuck it, this is my time.' I used to see all these pompous celebrities acting like divas and I thought I had to be more like that."

Exactly who was advising Michael on press matters at this time is unclear. But an ill-advised trip to a massage parlour in Manila in 2004 with Q magazine's Michael Odell resulted in an exposé that could not have been worse timed. He and Debbie had reconciled after an initial split and were trying to make the patched-up relationship work. But Odell's article appears to have been a final nail in his relationship's coffin.

"He wrote about what we talked about on a drinking night with the guys. And some things I didn't even say or do, he just wrote," Bublé says. "I read the story and I was devastated and embarrassed. My poor grandmother vomited. He could have chosen to make me look like a young lad who's just a little bit wild, a really nice kid who's just living his fantasy and loving it."

The experience of being 'turned over' by a publication that once led with a regular feature called 'Who The Hell Does… Think He Is?', which took a swing each month at a different celebrity who the magazine considered too 'up themselves', was a salutary one for Michael. "I learned my lesson," he said ruefully. "I learned that the writers are not your friends." The story was no longer poor guy makes good, but star riding for a fall…

As if all this wasn't enough, his name was constantly being associated with other women in the public eye. One was Cecelia Ahern, glamorous blonde daughter of Irish prime minister Bertie Ahern. Coincidentally, her elder sister Georgina was married to another pop star, Nicky Byrne of Irish boy band Westlife. Cecelia, who herself had briefly tasted pop stardom with girl group Shimma, was in a relationship with athlete David Keoghan, and when the pair unexpectedly split, her friendship with Michael was cited as a possible factor.

He had in fact met the young lady some eight months earlier on an Irish TV talk show, so it seemed some gossip columnist was working overtime in putting two and two together. The real reason was David's training regime in the run-up to the Athens Olympics and novelist Cecelia's demanding publishing deadlines – a career clash of the type that would occur more than once in Michael's own story.

Happily, while the headlines were unwelcome for Michael, given his recently rebuilt bridges with Debbie, Cecelia and David reconnected and, in December 2009, celebrated the birth of their first child.

So, with Debbie now part of his past, Michael was single again. But he soon found being footloose and fancy free was not his style. Having spent so long in a serious relationship, Michael felt the lack of a steady partner in whom he could confide – even if there was no lack of physical comforts on offer. "Yeah, I've slept with fans," he's admitted. "But there's a sad realisation when you think, 'I'm a celebrity, that's why'." Girls were adopting all kinds of subterfuge to reach him, including sending a stuffed teddy bear up to his hotel room that gave the girl's room number when its paw was touched!

But the next woman under whose spell Michael would fall was British actress Emily Blunt. The pair met backstage in Melbourne at the Australian television Logie Awards in 2005. Blunt was filming opposite Susan Sarandon and Sam Neill in the Australian thriller *Irresistible*, playing the role of a 'marriage-wrecking temptress'. Technically, that first meeting took place when both were still 'attached' to others. But when that changed, the relationship was set to take a more serious turn.

Michael invited her to one of his concerts in Los Angeles and the pair began dating shortly afterwards. "I wasn't in great shape mentally, nor was she. We'd both come out of long relationships," Bublé says. "We took it slowly, became friends first, which is something I've not done too often. And it's been great." Michael thought Blunt was a television producer working for the BBC when they met. But the truth was somewhat different.

Born in the London suburb of Roehampton in 1983 (and thus seven-and-a-half years Michael's junior), Emily was the daughter of a barrister and a teacher. She got her first break when still a student; a play she starred in at her sixth-form college went to the Edinburgh Festival, confirming her ambition to tread the boards.

Her breakthrough appearance came in 2004 as Tamsin, a 'well-educated, cynical and deceptive beauty' in *My Summer Of Love*. The following year saw her follow her uncle, Conservative member of Parliament Crispin Blunt, into the political world, but only on screen. She played the troubled only child of Labour spin doctor Gideon Warner, a role taken by veteran character actor Bill Nighy, in British TV drama *Gideon's Daughter*.

Having established who his new girlfriend *wasn't*, Michael did some further investigation. "First I thought she was some struggling actress like any girl you meet in LA. Then I saw her in *My Summer Of Love*. I got intimidated. This is not just an actor. She's a strong actor with incredible instincts. It's scary how good she is. Then I saw *Gideon's Daughter*... it wasn't a fluke."

When Emily won a Best Supporting Actress Golden Globe for *Gideon's Daughter*, Bublé was more than proud of his partner. "That was the greatest night of my career," he told the press. "For one day I got to feel like my family gets to feel. I understood what my mum and dad and grandparents say when they tell me they get more joy out of seeing me succeed than I do."

The pair moved together into Emily's $2.2 million home in Vancouver, although the demands of their different careers made time together relatively rare. While Michael promoted the release of second major-label album *It's Time*, Emily's stock was about to go through the roof as 2006 brought her best-known role opposite Meryl Streep and Anne Hathaway in *The Devil Wears Prada*.

Although Emily's two American co-stars would attract most of the publicity, Meryl Streep was impressed enough to pronounce her "the best young actress I've worked with in some time, perhaps ever."

Offers for further roles came flooding in and Emily would be a constant on the big screen for the next couple of years. She appeared in *The Jane Austen Book Club*, *The Young Victoria*, in which she played Queen Victoria in early adulthood, and *The Great Buck Howard* with Tom Hanks and John Malkovich. Hanks also co-starred with her in *Charlie Wilson's War*.

Still in her mid-twenties, the movie world was at the young woman's feet. But Emily had concerns as to her future direction. "When you've done a lot of period pieces and you're British," she mused, "you can get seriously pigeon-holed. 'English rose' is a character description I see a lot, and it makes me cringe. I'm far more drawn to playing off-the-wall people."

While Debbie Timuss had considered "the whole music thing a crock of shit", Emily took a keen interest in Michael's area of expertise. She had learned to play the cello when at school and could also sing, as she would prove when she provided background vocals on Bublé's cover of 'Me And Mrs Jones' on the *Call Me Irresponsible* album.

Indeed, Blunt had shown she could vocalise as soon as the pair met, Bublé telling the *Toronto Star:* "When I met her she said that her favourite song on the [*It's Time*] album was [the Nelly Furtado collaboration] 'Quando, Quando, Quando'. I said, 'Yeah right, go ahead and sing it.' She sang it, and I said, 'Oh, my God, you can really *sing*, girl.' It's really scary how talented she is."

Each was the other's biggest fan. "I get tears in my eyes when I see him onstage. It's overwhelming," Blunt told *People* magazine in 2007. The feeling was mutual. "Every time I see her on-screen, I fall in love with her all over again," Bublé said.

When Michael had been invited to meet her parents, he had also fallen in love with the whole family. Emily's father taught – or, more accurately, tried to teach – him the English sport of cricket, while her mother's dry sense of humour struck a chord with the Canadian. He also hit it off with Emily's younger siblings, two sisters and a teenage brother.

"The great thing," he said of the Blunts, "is that I can be myself with them – be rude, swear, whatever – and they just laugh." This, apparently, contrasted with the Timuss parents who, though "sweet and lovely", were also "very proper. I had to be on my best behaviour and couldn't always manage it." Michael clearly felt comfortable in this close family background that paralleled his own.

With roots like this, Michael and Emily's was more than just a celebrity relationship. And while the singer's still-ascending star had risen far above Debbie Timuss, here he was living with someone whose fame arguably equalled, and might soon exceed, his own. Pressure of work wouldn't help things either, as Michael told *People* magazine. "In my business it's tough to go out with another artist because you're never together. You're lucky if you can see the person once every two to three months."

Emily was, however, faithfully waiting in the wings in 2007 when Michael reprised his wedding-singer role on the French Riviera at the nuptials of one James Packer, the son of the late Australian media mogul Kerry Packer. Michael and his full band had been contracted to do a half-hour set, but he ended up doing an hour-and-a-half, because he felt "they'd been nice to me." The Australian wedding of the year included Tom Cruise and Katie Holmes among its guests, a fact that Emily, who had no idea who the Packers were, thought "a little bizarre".

The subject of marriage was bound to come up – and when Michael said in a Canadian radio interview that "I want to be the father of her kids", and went on to say, "I haven't proposed to her yet...[but] I'm sort of proposing through this interview," it seemed that things were set to move to another level. Michael's mother Amber was certainly championing a permanent union. "If he doesn't marry her, I'll *kill* him," she said. "But we'd find someone in the family to marry her because we're not letting her go, ever. She's just the best thing ever and they're perfect together."

But alarm bells rang not long after those remarks were made in early 2008, when another women, ex-model Tiffany Bromley, claimed that she had had an ongoing affair with Bublé for almost a decade. Then in June, Michael was shockingly quoted as saying he would never take Emily as his bride. "We will never be getting married," he told the *Daily Mirror*. "*Never*. I know I had indicated we would, but now it's a total no-no."

The writing was on the wall, and it came as little surprise when the end of the relationship was announced the following month by

Michael's representative Liz Rosenberg to gossip webmaster Perez Hilton. "Sadly, after three years, Michael and Emily have parted ways. They are both extraordinary people with huge talent. Let's wish them well."

Fortunately, Emily soon found her perfect partner in actor John Krasinski. The pair were introduced in November 2008 by Blunt's co-star in *The Devil Wears Prada,* Anne Hathaway, and quickly started dating. Blunt and Krasinski announced their engagement in August 2009, and they married in Como, Italy just under a year later. George Clooney was among the guests at an outdoor ceremony. Bublé was not present but sent his best wishes. "We talked and I congratulated her. Emily is amazing, so this guy also has to be."

He believed that if he hadn't been so open about their romance, he and Emily might still be together. "We were naive, I think," he told the *Providence Journal* newspaper. "We were both excited about the relationship, and we talked openly about it, and I think we both learned that when you give away even little things, they're not yours anymore. So I've learned just to keep my private life private."

In 2009, he revealed to *Seven* magazine that it took him quite a while to get over the relationship, describing it as "one of the worst and greatest things that ever happened to me". The break-up was, he said, "devastating. Emily is truly one of the most amazing and wonderful people that I've ever known. And really, even now I sit and I'm thrilled that I got a chance to be a part of someone's life who's touched so many lives and is so amazing.

"It's weird," he continued. "There's no more pain. There's feelings of hurt, but I'm just proud of her. And I'm still great friends with her brother, and I love her family to death. And it gave me an opportunity to take a good look at myself and to want to change, and to want to become a better guy."

The heartbreak of losing Emily Blunt was, perhaps, hardly comparable with the emotional turmoil Frank Sinatra went through when he had a brief and tempestuous marriage with Ava Gardner in the Fifties. But it seemed the three years Michael had spent with her weighed more heavily on him than the seven with first love Debbie Timuss.

In 2009, Bublé, offered his reasoned perspective on the heartache he had suffered on the demise of his relationship with Emily. "The point of it is to give us an opportunity to look at why it happened in the first place, and to try to make sure that, each time we go through another relationship, that we don't allow the same issues to affect us."

Although never publicly recognised, Tiffany Bromley appears to have played a part in the split. Certainly her claims, backed up with a naked photo of Bublé, were making headlines worldwide after being exclusively splashed in Canadian tabloid *The Globe*. "Michael is a cheater and a rat," said the 28-year-old. "We've made mad, passionate love a couple of times since he and Emily have been together."

Bromley was happy to list the effects fame and fortune had had on Michael. She believed they had turned him into a "self-obsessed jerk" who "uses swear words and colourful language", but she nevertheless gave him an "an 11 out of 10" rating in bed – and claimed he once suggested a threesome. "I told him, 'No way!' He said, 'Don't knock it till you've tried it. You don't know what you're missing.'"

Michael apparently saw himself "as a real ladies' man who could schmooze any women into bed, and had done so on tours," said Bromley, warming to her theme. "He told me I needed to loosen up. Many times he said, 'I have the best-looking penis.' He bragged about how it gave ultimate pleasure to women. I just ignored him. But he *was* good in bed."

Bromley alleged that Bublé sometimes smoked joints. "He always had a couple [of joints] in his wash bag ready to go. He insisted it was his way of winding down at the end of a day. He said he needed pot as a key part of his creativity. He said he could write his best songs with it."

Bromley also recalled that, as Buble's fame grew, so did his waistline. "It was part of Michael's routine to smoke at night. Then he always got hungry. He'd raid the hotel mini-bar and eat three or four Snickers bars." His ego was sizeable too, she claimed. "He often said to me, 'I'm the best living singer there is'."

Michael had never publicly proposed to Emily but had raised the subject of marriage in interviews, possibly to see what her reaction would be. Perhaps he was twice-shy after his attempt to paper over the cracks with Debbie, but he also said, in 2007, that he and Emily would laugh at news reports of their supposed engagement. At the same time, he commented that he was really "turned off reading celebrities gushing about each other. 'She's my snooky-wooky-pooky and I'm the luckiest man in the world!'"

Once the relationship had foundered, Michael accepted he had been in need of a wake-up call, "not a light little shake of 'wake up Mikey-pooh' – I needed a good kick in the head. I've been sleeping for a while, but I'm awake now." He described Emily as "a substantial person and amazing still. Top girl. Top class", and went on to describe what he looked for in a woman: "I don't want a pushover, I want a strong human being that doesn't put up with my bullshit. It turns me on actually."

But Buble was not to remain single for long, thanks to Argentinean actress, singer and model Luisana Lopilato. Born in May 1987, Luisana Loreley Lopilato de la Torre (to give her her full name) was 12 years Michael's junior, but had wasted little time in becoming Argentina's most famous actress. News of her association with an international superstar would, of course, spread her name across the globe at the click of a mouse.

Luisana's rise to fame began when she was talent-spotted in the street by a casting director at the age of six and, despite her mother's initial reservations, began a career in commercials. Her breakthrough role was that of Guivivere in the 2001 Argentine drama, *Un Amor En Moises Ville*. There was a problem, however. Luisana's character spoke in both Spanish and English, whereas the actress herself spoke only Spanish. Not willing to let the role slip away from her, Luisana didn't admit she spoke no English until all the Spanish-language scenes had been shot. She ultimately completed the job with the help of an English coach.

But Luisana is perhaps still best known in Argentina for her role as Luisana Maza in the popular children's television series *Chiquititas*, which she joined in 1999. The show, whose title translates as 'Little Angels', had a strong musical element that led to the cast staging a huge Broadway-style musical at Argentina's biggest theatre, Teatro Gran Rex, each summer. Luisana also appeared on four *Chiquititas* soundtrack albums issued over the following two years.

Over the next few years, Luisana would combine acting with a burgeoning musical career, often taking roles which offered the possiblity of both, as with the soap *Rebelde Way* (Rebel Way), about a group of students at a boarding school who formed a pop band called Erreway. This led to Luisana and her co-stars releasing three studio albums under that name – *Señales (2002)*, *Tiempo (2003)* and *Memoria (2004)* – which together sold over five million copies worldwide.

Luisana also found time to build a third career as a model, in which her unique combination of fashionable beauty and girl-next-door charm led her to become the face of sexy underwear brand Promesse between 2006 and 2010. She has also modelled for the 47 Street clothing line, and at the time of writing is involved in campaigns for the Marcela Koury lingerie brand and L'Oréal Elvive cosmetics.

After failed romances with sometime co-stars Felipe Colombo and Mariano Martínez, Luisana would eventually meet Bublé in 2008 at one of his gigs. "They met at a party the record company threw for him after his show in Buenos Aires," a friend told *People* magazine. "The head of the label wanted to introduce Michael to Argentina's most famous actress. When he met her, he said it was love at first sight."

Michael recalled their first meeting to British newspaper *The Sun*, and revealed the romance almost never happened at all. "I spotted her in the crowd and thought she was the most beautiful woman I'd ever laid eyes on, but she came backstage with this good-looking dude and I assumed it was her boyfriend.

"The other problem was that I don't speak Spanish and she had no English. But the guy did, so I just spoke to him. I was a bit nervous because of how beautiful she was. The more I drank, the more I made things worse. I was saying to him, 'You're a good-looking dude', and 'You guys are a good-looking couple.' I later found out she was on the phone to her mother the whole time saying, 'Bublé's gay. He's hitting on my friend.' She couldn't believe it."

Once the initial confusion had been resolved the pair hit it off, despite both the language barrier and the fact that they had each recently emerged from relationships (hers with tennis player Juan Monaco). The couple initially tried to keep their romance low-key, but Luisana travelled with him when he appeared on David Letterman's US talk show and when he performed for Australian television in front of the Sydney Opera House in late 2009.

It was only a year since he'd told *Entertainment Tonight Canada* that "I'll go home and I'll curl up in a ball and I'll cry. I'm not kidding. I'll just cry", following his split from Emily Blunt. Yet already the possibility of a permanent union with his Latin American lovely Luisana had been mooted. "It's too early to tell," he had told TV channel WENN in October, "but she's a good soul and I love her family, so we'll see!"

The couple spent New Year 2009–10 in Hawaii, where they "had a great time", according to a friend. Her appearance shortly thereafter in the video for 'Haven't Met You Yet', the first single from Michael's fourth major label release, *Crazy Love*, signalled to the world that the pair were taking their new-found relationship seriously.

However, despite telling the world they were for keeps, there was still surprise in some quarters when it was revealed the pair were engaged to be married – not least because it was announced through Bublé's publicist in a somewhat gushing press release.

"Michael proposed to his girlfriend, Luisana, in November [2010] in front of her family in Argentina," Bublé's representative Liz Rosenberg told celebrity magazine *People*. "They're ecstatic. They're adorable, in love and laugh all day long. He's very proud to be engaged to her." The deal was sealed by a diamond engagement ring from Vancouver jeweller Minichiello that Michael gave her. It became even more significant when he revealed that he had designed the setting himself.

Michael and Luisana planned on having two weddings – one in Argentina and one in Canada. He told *ET Canada*, "We are doing one in Argentina and that's for her close family, and then we are doing one in Vancouver."

He revealed his nerves, meanwhile, to UK breakfast show *Daybreak*. "It's only four months away and now I'm starting to get a little nervous! The truth is I know that for a lot of women, this is what they dream of – that day – and I know that that's a big deal for them in their life and they want it to be perfect. I'm a boy, I didn't grow up thinking about my wedding day, so for me, I just want it to be good for her."

But if the pair were planning a low-key ceremony in Lopilato's home country, they would be in for a shock. Luckily, Michael knew all about his bride-to-be's status with the Argentinean press. "The paparazzi will stand in front of the car and then they'll lie on the car so you can't go anywhere. And there are tons of them and they chase you on their bikes. It's amazing. It's like a movie or something."

Michael joked that they had considered setting the date for April 29, 2011 before deciding that the nuptials of a certain British royal couple might just steal the show. "I was going to do it… but figured I wouldn't get any press," he quipped.

Instead, they left William and Kate to enjoy their day uncontested. The date for Michael and Luisana's ceremony was fixed for a month earlier, March 31. It was, as Michael had said, just for Luisana's close friends and family. The pair tied the knot in a civil ceremony in Buenos Aires – but while things were kept deliberately low-key inside, fans packed the immediate area outside the hall, eager to catch a glimpse of their idol. This time, though, it wasn't Michael in his trademark sharp grey suit who was the centre of attention but Luisana, resplendent in silver heels and a purple dress by designer Sylvie Burstin, who joyously hurled her bouquet of orchids into the crowd.

The second leg of the Argentinean celebrations occurred at the Villa María palace in Cañuelas over the weekend, with 300 guests attending. However, while the resort was bustling with friends and family wishing the happy couple well, opportunistic thieves capitalised on the situation by breaking into the couple's Buenos Aires home. But Lopilato was in defiant mood, reportedly telling officers when they broke the news, "I will not let this ruin the happiest day of my life."

With Michael's popularity at a high, having just taken home his third Grammy, it would be easy to assume Luisana – the 17th sexiest woman in the world according to the Spanish edition of *FHM* magazine – might not be a favourite with his hordes of female fans, but he revealed that it was, in fact, the other way around. "In South America she is a massive star and I get the feeling some people – perhaps her fans – don't like me. And the media there have said terrible things about me. It's a shame. I love the place and the people, and she's a great person."

Meanwhile, Michael's fans, for the most part, were happy for the couple. Those in attendance to witness the happy occasion threw rice and red rose petals, while the reception in cyberspace was equally rosy. "[I'm] happy... I guess... more, sad [that] he's off the market," wrote one, while another simply wished "huge congratulations to Michael & Lu, they look so happy & beautiful together." As for Luisana, she kept her message for her 500,000 Facebook and Twitter fans short and sweet. "How beautiful it all was!" she wrote.

Many would be forgiven for thinking that Michael and Luisana's honeymoon would be set on an idyllic beach with white sand and blue sea, the pictures strewn across national newspapers across the world. The reality, however, would be rather different. After a few days in Venice, the pair would head off to Africa to conduct charity work, seeking a meaningful start to the rest of their lives together.

"We're gonna go and help kids and dig ditches," he told the Australian *Daily Telegraph*. "It's not my idea – it's her idea! I wanted to go to Paris, and shopping in Rome!" Ever the joker, it looked like Michael had found the perfect woman to complement him. Everyone hoped it would be a case of third time lucky. But the first precious days of married life were to be lived out in the full glare of the media spotlight.

When Michael and his new bride reached Venice, their space was immediately invaded by photographers, mirroring the frenzied press attention that had surrounded them in Buenos Aires. Unlike many celebrities who use the paparazzi and the tabloids to gain fame, Michael was less than happy to be the target of long lenses. And while he laughed and smiled at the Venezian photographers, he would clearly have preferred them to leave his life.

"It makes me wonder sometimes when people who were created by the tabloids start to complain about their lack of privacy and they don't want them to film them anymore. But I wasn't built by the paparazzi or tabloids – they had absolutely nothing to do with the success I've had. I've worked hard, I had integrity, I put my head down and I did what I had to do."

He hid under a black baseball cap, while he and Luisana both sported shades as they travelled the waterways in a Venetian taxi. The following day saw them take a romantic gondola ride. Pictures of Michael cradling Luisana in his arms flashed around the world – young love sells celebrity magazines, and the showbiz world's latest celebrity couple were clearly hot stuff.

The pair would have to synchronise their calendars and make the most of what time they had together between professional commitments. Having wrapped up shooting on the soap opera *Alguien Que Me Quiera*, Luisana then relocated to Los Angeles, where she would star in an ABC series called *The River* set to premiere later in 2011. She was also awaiting the premiere of her first internationally released movie – the Spanish thriller *Predeterminados*, directed by Jordi Arencón, in which she played Vera.

As the Bublés returned to the groom's home turf for a second set of nuptials in May, Michael was sporting a healthy growth of beard. The reason was the National Hockey League playoffs, and it was clear Luisana would have to get used to this, as well as to Michael's ice-hockey obsession. "I'm not shaving till these boys lose. So I'm not shaving, and I don't care, as you can see by my incredibly thick beard. I'm going to be watching it every chance I get!"

He had big-screen TVs set up at the reception so he and his friends wouldn't miss any of the action. So if Luisana hadn't realised by that point that she would be sharing her new, hirsute groom with a bunch of sweaty male hockey fans, she would pretty soon have her eyes opened.

In the long term, the opportunity was clearly there for Michael and Luisana to become one of the north American celebrity scene's golden couples, alongside Brad and Angelina, Tom and Katie, David and Victoria, and the like. It seemed clear that Luisana was setting her sights on US TV stardom, and with her combination of talent and good looks few would bet against her achieving it.

One problem, however, was her less than fluent command of the English language. Michael had already admitted that she couldn't speak English when they started dating and talked to him using a dictionary. And while the makers of *Un Amor En Moises Ville* had considered her assets worth the trouble of coaching her through the language barrier, the prospect of dubbing her into English certainly limited Luisana's television and movie chances in the short term, her stunning looks notwithstanding.

In 2009 she was rumoured to be in the running to play Tanya, the leader of the Denali coven in the *Twilight* saga. Whether or not she met with *Eclipse* director David Slade is unknown, but the role was not forthcoming. However, her appearance in the previously mentioned ABC series *The River*, the pilot episode for which was shot in Puerto Rico, seemed likely to give her a break.

The River tells the story of wildlife expert and TV personality Emmet Cole who goes missing deep in the Amazon while filming a television show. His family, friends and crew set out on a journey to find him. With executive producer Steven Spielberg and *Paranormal Activity* creator Oren Peli involved, this seemed set to be a highlight of the ABC network's schedule. Filming was scheduled to take place in the Amazon-like wilds of Hawaii.

Meanwhile, Michael and Luisana made their television debut as a couple in a lifestyle show, *Cooking With The Stars*. Michael credited his mother and grandma as culinary inspirations, revealing that they didn't use cookbooks but "did it by feel". His suitably Italian trademark dish was "a nice vegetarian risotto" with asparagus and chicken stock. "It takes a couple of hours, but with a couple of glasses of wine you're ready to go."

Whether Luisana would convert him to more exotic fare in the couple's kitchen remained to be seen. But it was clear that the world's appetite for Michael had yet to be satisfied. And if his new bride was now part of the deal, so much the spicier...

CHAPTER 8

The Future

If you've read this far, it can probably be assumed you are a Michael Bublé fan. But have you ever tried to convince a non-believer and found it hard to put his appeal into words?

When David Roberts, editor of the *Guinness Book Of Hit Singles And Albums* and one of several commentators impressed by Bublé's British success, was asked to sum up just that, he suggested it was "down to timing, in two senses. First his breakthrough with 'Haven't Met You Yet' was such a big success mostly because there was no other easy-listening class act around at the time. Secondly, apart from his obvious charms for the ladies, his musical timing as a singer is so on the money. If you created a perfect-pitch singer on a computer that somehow didn't end up sounding manufactured, it would be Michael Bublé.

"He sings like Frank Sinatra and looks like George Clooney. In the UK we have some great male vocalists, but we just don't seem to be able to produce smooth operators like him."

But for how long is this smooth operator set to stay at the top? The answer is probably as long as he gets a kick out of performing live and has the motivation to take his music to the worldwide following he currently enjoys. For even considering his impressive recording career to date, with quantum leaps at every album, it seems certain that the one thing that really drives Michael Bublé is his rapport with a live audience. It's something he has cultivated ever since his days at the café's bars and roadhouses like the BaBalu, where he often had to silence the buzz of conversation so he could be heard.

Now people pay an increasing amount of money to see him, usually in respectful near-silence – and often from a seat in the least intimate of aircraft hangars. This, of course, was a by-product of success, but it posed a new challenge for the Canadian: how to reduce the large venues to an intimate size and how to establish a rapport with his audience similar to the one he had always enjoyed? The answer was simple if unexpected… getting his lighting man to turn the house lights up!

Seeing his audience in their thousands didn't make him nervous, he explained – quite the opposite. "I can't give them that much respect. What would happen if I did that, is that I would get really nervous and I would let the moment get the best of me, so what I have to do is, I have to think to myself, 'Just go, do my job, enjoy it, take in the moment, feel the connection of all those people', because that is the coolest part about my life."

Audience interaction is the name of the game, and it is what makes a Michael Bublé show different from any other ticket on offer. Recreating this night after night, however, can be tough. "I need to always keep in my head how lucky I am that I get to have these two hours with these people. You know, you have 15 or 16 shows and you do four and you're excited, and then you start to float through the next three. You don't mean to do it; it's not about having any disrespect to your audience, but you're just human and you do it."

The responsibility to his audience to justify the ticket price would never leave the shoulders of this fisherman's son. Even the challenge of the 12,500-seat Wembley Arena in London, where he filmed part of a 2010 TV documentary, failed to phase him. "It's pretty tiny compared to what to what I usually play so this feels very intimate." That is an indication of the scale of success he now enjoyed.

And part of the enjoyment, for Michael Bublé, was the danger, the unpredictability of it all. He was now a household name like Sinatra, Martin and Davis. Yet, as with the Rat Pack, there was a side of him that loved to live dangerously. His habit of going out into the crowd when performing raised the stakes and could lead him into trouble. It only takes one deranged individual eager to make a name for himself to bring down the curtain, maybe for good. And Michael very nearly found that out one night when performing in Virginia.

"Sometimes, for whatever reason, people will try to take a swing at you," he recalled later of a male audience member who turned feral. "I could hear him screaming as the crowd enveloped me, I could hear him screaming at me and I kind of turned and, as I turned, his fist came and he just missed me."

As Bublé retreated to the safety of the stage, his attacker followed him. And though the singer didn't realise it at first, the man had a deadly weapon. "He had a garrote, do you know what that is? They use it to cut your throat. So the FBI picked him up and said, 'What are you doing here?' And he said, 'I have come to kill Michael Bublé, God told me to kill Michael Bublé.' They said why, and he said, 'Because he stole music from black people!' I mean, I understand there are a lot of reasons to want to kill me, but that is *not* one of them!"

Michael's way of handling his audience is light and attractive, but it could also lead to other kinds of trouble. At one show, for instance, he encouraged them to stand up – and if anyone sitting behind complained, to tell them where to go, or words to that effect. His intention was clear – to get everyone in the house up and dancing. But what would happen if members of his audience were unable to stand for health reasons? Sadly, at least one such person received the advice dispensed from the stage by the star. Not what he had intended at all.

Such a *faux pas* was unretractable in a live scenario but, as has already been recounted, corrective action was possible when, starring in his own *Audience With…* show, Michael managed to answer some of the audience questions in a manner the broadcasting authorities considered unsuitable for a Saturday-night prime-time TV audience. A number of retakes were necessary to 'save his reputation'.

Was Michael a rock 'n' roller trapped in a crooner's body? Was there an inner Axl Rose struggling to get out? It seems not. When asked by TV presenter Steve Mulhern on *An Audience With…* to name his childhood heroes, his answer stayed close to home. "In all honesty my father and grandfather – and they're *still* my heroes. I think if I turn out half as good as those gentlemen then I'm on the right path." His upbringing and the work ethic bred into him at an early age would clearly never leave him.

Happily, grandpa Mitch was still around to share in Michael's success, though a heart condition meant he couldn't come to the shows any more. They made a habit of speaking each night, no matter where in the world Michael might be, and every night he would pay tribute to his musical mentor on stage. He couldn't conceive of the inevitable day his grandfather would not be around to take his nightly call. "I don't want to think about that… the thought is too devastating. I know it's going to happen one day, and I don't know how I'm going to deal with it."

Like an athlete, a top-line showbiz performer needs to keep him or herself in shape – and there's no doubt that Michael's current slimline body is part of the package. Yet since his romance with Luisana began in 2008, he had been pictured more than once in swimming trunks on the beach. And some cruel caption writers suggested he was exhibiting the beginnings of a paunch.

Whether it's due to Bublé's Italian background or not, he admits to enjoying his food. But just as he eased off smoking to save his voice, he has watched his calorie intake since his major-label signing to ensure he can fit into those trademark sharp suits. How long he will consider the sacrifice worthwhile is open to debate. But headlines on one gossip website that greeted a sunshine break in Barbados in January 2011 – "Michael Bublé shows off man boobs; housewives weep in unison" – were somewhat unnecessary.

If Michael occasionally craved a nine-to-five existence with domestic bliss on evenings and weekends (not to mention the BBQ!), he needed look no further than his sister Crystal. She had married insurance broker Lanny McVeigh in April 2005 and was enjoying an idyllic time. The happy couple had been introduced by Lewis and Amber, Lanny having been a fisherman in a former life. Michael had reprised his role of wedding singer at the church to serenade them with his version of Stevie Wonder's 'You And I' before sending them all-expenses paid to Vegas on their honeymoon.

Fast forwarding six years to May 2011, Lanny and former actress Crystal had diversified to take a third share in Displace Hashery, a seafood restaurant at Vancouver's Fourth and Blenheim. Their opening gambit was predictable – get big brother to make an appearance and catch the fish-and-chip crowd in large numbers! This he was happy to do, though whether he sampled the signature dishes – Drunken Fish 'n' Chips at $16, and Crab Burger at $8 – is unknown. Luisana came too, and the local press were quick to liken the 200-seat venue to the similarly sized BaBalu he'd helped fill... was it really a dozen years earlier?

Michael's other sister had also married. She was now Brandee Ubels, and she had a fulfilling career as a teacher of special needs children. She was therefore unlikely to feel overshadowed by her brother, while Crystal was also admirably level-headed about their relative levels of fame. She did, however, occasionally quip that she could remember when she was the bigger earner...

The Future

Nowadays, of course, Michael was very much the local celebrity, with Vancouver anxious to claim him as their own. He had long buried the bad memories of Cariboo Hill High School where a plaque, presented by his father Lewis with much celebratory fanfare, proclaimed the past presence of their most famous pupil. Likewise, the British Columbia Entertainment Hall of Fame announced him as their key inductee for 2009, the pavement on Granville Street – Vancouver's Entertainment Row – receiving a new paving stone in his honour. Again, this was just a stone's throw from the BaBalu, situated at the junction of Granville and Nelson.

Beach pictures apart, Michael was now firmly a darling of the mainstream media, as was proved in 2008 when *Chatelaine* magazine approached him to become their cover star. Nothing unusual about that, you might have thought – but he was treading in the footsteps of only two men, former prime minister Pierre Trudeau and hockey icon Wayne Gretzky, to have received and accepted a similar invitation. Given the women's-interest publication was first published in 1928, that's no mean feat.

"I'm not a big magazine guy," he smiled, when asked if he had actually read the magazine before gracing its pages. He wouldn't allow himself to be compared with the two nationally revered male figures he had followed, but suggested the question be asked again in another 20 years – the answer of a man with a game plan career-wise.

Despite his cover-star status, at the end of the day Michael Bublé is just an ordinary person, if one possessed of unusual talents. That was underlined when his home in Argentina was burgled while he was getting married. Had Michael got hold of the wrongdoer, it is likely he might have dished out some rough justice, if an incident a few years previously was any guide.

When he had witnessed a cyclist spit in the face of an old lady in her car in his home town of Vancouver, Michael immediately got out of his own car to sort the cyclist out. "My instinct was that was not OK, threatening an old lady." But when Bublé had calmed down, his next action was self-preservation. "I called my manager and told him what had happened in case the man knew who I was, in case this came out in the papers."

He went on to claim he was worried about his family "reading this stuff". But if you were surprised he had the bottle to get involved, then you have misjudged the man. "I think [people] assume that maybe I'm soft – [because of my] genre of music, people categorise me. I'm not some hard-assed, bad-assed motherfucker. But I'm not soft."

But would maturity, success and personal fulfillment soften him? With Michael Bublé now safely spoken for in terms of love and marriage, it seemed he might find it advisable to tone down the intimate chat with his live audience. Not that he'd necessarily agree…

"It is nice for me to speak about my own personal life in front of the audience; I think it makes me a lot less predatory as an entertainer. You've got girls screaming at you, [and] there are two ways you can handle that. You can take it all in and act like you are that sex symbol, or you can take it with humility and you can laugh at yourself."

Meanwhile, meeting Luisana appeared to have helped him come to terms with his predatory side. "I'm a happier guy in my life now, I have more respect for myself, and I like myself. That comes with me, you know: this is who I really am and that comes out on stage with me. If you're happier in your life, that'll show."

As far as his 2011 work schedule went, Michael had been holed up in the Record Plant, Los Angeles, for the first months of the year recording what his friend from the UK's *The X Factor*, Dermot O'Leary, somewhat indiscreetly revealed on radio would be a Christmas album. While Michael had gone down the seasonal route before, in 2003, he had yet to cut a full-length album of such songs – and it was surely something his fans would hope to find in their stockings come the end of 2011. It would be followed by a 'regular' album sometime in 2012.

Inbetween recording and preparing for his wedding, Michael also found time to pop across town to Capitol Studios where Tony Bennett was cutting a follow-up to 2006's *Duets*, on which Michael had also appeared. His return booking saw him line up alongside the likes of kd lang, Norah Jones and Josh Groban.

Live work, too, had continued, after a suitable period of honeymooning. The second Stateside leg of his Crazy Love Tour was set to commence on June 1 at Austin, Texas's Frank Erwin Centre. By the time it ended up 24 days later at the less than romantically named AMSOIL Arena in Duluth, Minnesota, it would have wended its way, with no more than one day's rest per week, through Providence, Rhode Island, Memphis, Tennessee and Atlantic City, New Jersey. Seventeen dates in total, needless to say, all sold out in minutes; Canadian dates were already being booked for August in British Columbia and Edmonton.

Of course, no matter how big you get there is always competition coming up on the rails. Michael was amused to be bracketed with one Justin Bieber, the latest teen idol, who came to public attention in 2010. Apart from both being Canadian, Bublé reasoned, they had little in common. Bieber had found management and, through them, won a recording contract by the very 21st-century method of posting performance videos of himself on Internet video channel YouTube.

"My country is proud of him," said Michael when quizzed at a press conference. "He's one of us; I actually really like him – he's a really talented kid. Am I going to work with him? I don't know, but I saw the trailer for the movie he has coming out and it was actually a really cool promo. I'm proud of him."

He then jokingly added a sinister dimension to the young singer's rise. "I've said it before and I'll say it again; there's something happening here that you guys don't talk about – and that's because you don't know. But I'll break it to you; while you Americans are sitting there getting fat, us Canadians are ready to take over. We're plotting; we've got Bieber, me, Celine, Alanis… You're absolutely fucked when we come!"

He was keen to underline the fact that their respective rises to fame bore no comparison; Bieber's rocket ride to YouTube stardom was quite different to the dues Michael had slogged to pay. "He's absolutely gigantic and he's a talented kid. We're Canadian and that's probably where the similarities end – I just didn't have the same path [as him]."

He reflected on how taking that route to the top would have been a lot easier, but at the age of 17 he would have been ill-equipped to withstand the pressures that came with stardom. "The truth is, I wouldn't have been ready for this kind of celebrity at 25, and I proved it over and over again by doing stupid things well into my early thirties! I'm 35 now and I'm *still* doing stupid things! I hope that when he's 35, 45 or 55 he still has a great career, but it's a difficult thing to do; we've seen what happens to a lot of teen stars. It can be tough knowing that your greatest years are behind you."

But Bublé has managed to avoid pinning his hopes on trends and trifles, opting for the safer middle of the road. This offers him a multitude of diversions along the way, and many believe television will be one of them. His easy manner and engaging personality make him a natural to follow the likes of his mentor Michael Parkinson into the interviewer's chair. Just as his music found its target audience in the United Kingdom through daytime TV shows like *Richard And Judy, Des And Mel* and *This Morning*, so he could easily flip roles and become the genial host.

He's certainly got the gift of the gab and this, plus his open personality and genuine interest in people, is the perfect combination.

The Future

Appearances on such shows as America's *Tonight Show With Jay Leno* and Britain's *Paul O'Grady Show* had demonstrated how easily he could hold his own with the big names, and it is clear Michael and the camera are the closest of friends.

Judging by his affinity with Britain's *The X Factor*, Michael would also be a perfect talent-show judge. He was entranced by the discovery of middle-aged Scots singing superstar Susan Boyle on *Britain's Got Talent*, and his response suggested he could happily line up alongside Simon Cowell at the judges' table. "I was cynical and critical because I had never seen her in that first show where she comes up and says, 'I want to be a singer' and the audience looks at her and says, 'Oh, *please!*' I got goosebumps.

"It really is a beautiful, beautiful story. It gives me faith in the human condition that we still have that kind of feeling that we actually want the good guy to win."

Like many stars who make it, Michael has shown himself keen to give back to those less fortunate than himself. One of his major commitments was to become an ambassador for the British Columbia Children's Hospital Foundation and their Campaign for BC Children. Having been a patient there himself when younger, it was a cause he took easily to his heart, saying, "Whatever I can do to help, I will do it."

Given his warm and close relationship with his Australian fans, Michael was particularly upset when the continent was stricken by natural disaster in early 2009. He pledged a donation of AUS$50,000 to the victims of the Black Saturday bushfires in Victoria, Australia.

And March 2011 saw him again make a contribution to those less fortunate than himself. He gifted an alternate version of 'Hold On' to *Songs For Japan*, a compilation of hits and classic tracks issued to benefit those affected by the earthquake and tsunami the country had just suffered. All proceeds went to the Japanese Red Cross Society (JRCS) to support its disaster relief efforts.

Someone who had played a major role in Michael's early rise to fame was Beverly Delich, and her return to the entertainment scene was celebrated by Michael himself. The seven years she had mentored and guided his career had culminated in her relocating to Los Angeles for a year, before passing the Bublé baton to other hands. Beverly had then taken time off to enjoy quality time with her recently arrived grandchildren, but had recently responded to requests to take on new up-and-coming artists. In her own words, "Utilising the tools and experience gained from working alongside the moguls... David Foster, Humberto Gatica and Paul Anka... I was up for the challenge of guiding and shaping the careers of new artists."

David Foster was happy to endorse her capabilities on the website of her company, Silver Lining Management. "Any artist who is lucky enough to have Beverly representing them will be shortcutting their road to success, if that is their destiny. She works from a place of complete honesty, integrity and class that is very rare in this business. She is also my friend and whenever she calls to get my opinion, I am there right away. She knows the difference between good, bad and more importantly, great... That gets my attention every time."

As if to guard against the possibility that fame might one day dry up and force him to return to that calling, Michael continued to invest in non-musical ventures such as the Vancouver Giants hockey team and the Tsawwassen Golf & Country Club. The latter – the name means 'looking towards the sea' – is on the British Columbian coast minutes from both the Vancouver International Airport, and the US border; very much Bublé's home territory.

Winter 2011 saw it closed for extensive construction work, which was intended to create a residential community comprising over 400 apartments and family dwellings, and a new clubhouse with a publicly accessible spa and gym. All this, as the plush promotional video had it, "situated on the edge of the world".

The Future

The project, complete with an upgraded, redesigned and expanded par-70 golf course, was scheduled for completion by 2016. It's uncertain whether Michael planned a round or two himself or whether the investment was strictly with a view to financial gain.

The Vancouver Giants, of course, is another matter entirely. His acquisition of a minority stake in December 2008 was the realisation of a lifetime dream. He rated it "the most prestigious move of my life" and insisted that he would not attempt to interfere in team matters. "As long as they don't tell me which songs to record, I promise I ain't gonna tell them who to put on the ice," he laughed.

The man who invited his investment was Ron Toigo who, uncoincidentally, was a long-time resident of Tsawwassen and managing director of the company developing the golf club there. Speaking of Michael's involvement in the hockey franchise, he said, "Having someone of Michael's stature get involved at the ownership level is a real statement on the strength of the Vancouver Giants brand, and that of the Western Hockey League as a whole. We're very excited to welcome Michael to the organisation, and look forward to having his energy and enthusiasm in the Giants family."

Michael added, "I couldn't be more thrilled to be a part of such a wonderful team, management and ownership – a group of winners!"

Michael generously shared his shareholding with father Lewis as a thank-you gesture. So not one but two Bublé faces adorned the Giants website, alongside fellow co-owners Sultan Thiara, Pat Quinn and former hockey legend Gordie Howe. Lewis's biography was more revealing than that of his son's in showing how far he had come since those full-time fishing days.

"Lewis is a long time director and vice president of the Board of Gulf & Fraser Financial Group and was named by Parks Canada as their Pacific Coast advisor for the Creation of National Marine Conservation Areas. As well, he is a director of Pacific

Coast Fishermen's Mutual Marine Insurance Company and is an appointee to the Pacific Region Advisory Council on Marine Oil Spill Response. He was also a long-time director and chairman of the BC Salmon Marketing Council."

With outside interests taking up more of his time and attention, not to mention his recent marriage, there was of course a danger that Michael might look to scale back on his musical activities. Looking at the competition, there was no reason why he should be obliged to continue his career at rock-star pace, anxious to cash in on every second of that mythical 15 minutes of fame.

After all, with singers in his field making a habit of growing old gracefully – the 85-year-old Tony Bennett being a case in point – there was no reason Michael Bublé couldn't, God willing, look forward to another four decades or more of music-making. He could certainly afford to pace himself, let a TV special or two do the travelling for him, and settle back to enjoy all married life had to offer.

But that wasn't something he was considering just now. "It's hard even to project forward to being 40," he complained, when quizzed about his future plans. Although he admitted to a responsibility to keep the Great American Songbook alive, the man who had started by self-confessedly mimicking Connick, Bennett and Sinatra had now found his own voice. Yet how much of that could truly be his, when he was singing others' songs?

"A big part of who I am, is an interpreter," he insisted. "It's a big part of what makes me who I am. I mean, I'm so in love with these songs; these are some of the greatest songs ever written and far after I'm gone, they'll still be alive, and they'll still move people, and they'll still be a soundtrack to people's lives. So I'll continue to keep doing what I was built to do – interpret the greatest songs that were ever written and to try and write some of my own that can try their best to match up to those great ones."

The Future

So it seemed his gradual evolution on record would continue, with maybe a couple of originals on each album and possibly more self-production without edging David Foster out of the studio door completely. It also seemed likely he would continue collaborating with Bob Rock, particularly as the pair now shared management – though an easy-listening medley of Mötley Crüe anthems appeared unlikely!

It was David Foster who had pointed out a truth when he said, "Harry Connick Jr opened the door wide, and then walked away from it to do movies and other things." That had left a vacancy for Michael Bublé to fill, and it seemed he was set to occupy the post of hip crooner until or unless he opted to vacate it. Would a change in his personal situation, such as fatherhood, be such a catalyst? Children would certainly seem more than a possibility, given his own happy family background.

Amber Bublé was a young mother, barely 20 when she had Michael, and he has often spoken warmly of the idea of fatherhood. He would recall his mother taking him out of school so they could spend time together in McDonald's in the guise of a 'dentist's appointment'. "I'm very close to my family, and I like women who have the same values," he has said in previous interviews.

He had been indiscreet enough when romancing Emily Blunt to state publicly that he would happily be the father of her babies. It never happened, of course, but the prospect of touring the world with his offspring growing up out of sight hardly seems a scenario he is likely to be comfortable with.

When exactly the right time for creating a family of little Bublés might be, of course, is a debatable point. With Luisana seemingly intent on making her mark in English-speaking America, the idea of a 12-to-18-month baby hiatus is almost unthinkable – and when your looks are your fortune, having a child is, in any case, a calculated gamble.

In 2010, Michael admitted he and Luisana had started the discussion of potential names, and joked that she wanted to name their offspring after characters from Stephenie Meyer's hit teen-vampire series, *Twilight*.

"I came up with some hypothetical names and I didn't like the names, but she came up with… Bella Bublé," he laughed. "I swear to God, she kept coming up with these names, and she kept saying, 'Bella', [or] 'I like Edward.' And then I realised, I think she's talking about… *Twilight*."

Michael then stated he "absolutely" wanted to have children some day and had every intention of being a good father. "I think nobody knows until you do it, and apparently when you do it, all of a sudden you just make it right."

So what keeps singing superstar Michael Bublé grounded as he faces his future? He was asked the question by his *X Factor* pal, Dermot O'Leary, and chose to make a joke of it. In fact, given John Lennon's *faux pas* in the Sixties when he said The Beatles were "bigger than Jesus", he very nearly put his foot in it before recovering.

"I am quite massive – I think worldwide is a bit of an understatement, I would say I'm universal, even! I'm actually more popular than Jesus at this point – not Jesus Christ, but the one that Madonna's been dating! But when it gets serious, I think my good-lookingness and my intelligence is what keeps me humble."

As long as that continues, Michael Bublé's fans are likely to continue worshipping at his feet…

Michael Bublé Discography

ALBUMS

Michael Bublé
  Released: February 11, 2003
  Label: 143 / Reprise

  Fever (3:51)/Moondance (4:13)/Kissing A Fool (4:34)/For Once in My Life (2:32)/How Can You Mend A Broken Heart (3:54)/Summer Wind (2:55)/You'll Never Find Another Love Like Mine (4:04)/Crazy Little Thing Called Love (3:09)/Put Your Head On My Shoulder (4:26)/Sway (3:08)/The Way You Look Tonight (4:37)/Come Fly With Me (3:30)/That's All (3:59)

It's Time
  Released: February 15, 2005
  Label: 143 / Reprise

  Feeling Good (3:57)/A Foggy Day (In London Town)(2:31)/You Don't Know Me (4:14)/Quando, Quando, Quando [duet with Nelly Furtado] (4:45)/Home (3:45)/Can't Buy Me Love (3:14)/

The More I See You (3:47)/Save The Last Dance For Me (3:38)/Try A Little Tenderness (4:05)/How Sweet It Is (To Be Loved by You) (2:58)/A Song For You [duet with Chris Botti] (4:42)/I've Got You Under My Skin (3:40)/You And I (3:55)

Call Me Irresponsible
Released: May 1, 2007
Label: 143 / Reprise

The Best Is Yet To Come (3:05)/It Had Better Be Tonight (Meglio Stasera) (3:06)/Me And Mrs Jones [duet with Emily Blunt] (4:33)/I'm Your Man (4:59)/Comin' Home Baby [duet with Boyz II Men] (3:27)/Lost (3:40)/Call Me Irresponsible (3:16)/Wonderful Tonight [duet with Ivan Lins] (4:12)/Everything (3:31)/I've Got The World On A String (2:47)/Always On My Mind (4:30)/That's Life (4:15)/Dream (5:06)

Other versions:
Call Me Irresponsible – Fan Edition exclusive to MichaelBuble.com
Call Me Irresponsible – Special Edition

Special Edition Bonus Track
L.O.V.E. (2:50)

Fan Edition Bonus Tracks
L.O.V.E. (2:50)/Orange Coloured Sky (3:30)

Tour Edition Bonus CD
Stuck In The Middle With You (3:37)/Lost (Pop Mix) (3:39)/Home (Pop Mix) (3:41)/Orange Coloured Sky (3:28)/Everything (Bob Rock Mix) (3:29)/Let It Snow! Let It Snow! Let It Snow! (2:06)/The Christmas Song (4:14)/White Christmas (3:57)

Crazy Love

Released: October 9, 2009
Label: 143 / Reprise

Cry Me A River (4:14)/All Of Me (3:07)/Georgia On My Mind (3:08)/Crazy Love (3:31)/Haven't Met You Yet (4:05)/All I Do Is Dream Of You (2:32)/Hold On (4:05)/Heartache Tonight (3:52)/You're Nobody Till Somebody Loves You (3:07)/Baby (You've Got What It Takes) [feat. Sharon Jones & The Dap-Kings] (3:20)/At This Moment (4:35)/Stardust [feat. Naturally 7] (3:13)/Whatever It Takes [feat. Ron Sexsmith, bonus track] (4:35)

Crazy Love (Hollywood Edition)

Released: October 18, 2010
Label: 143 / Reprise

CD1

Cry Me A River (4:14)/All Of Me (3:07)/Georgia On My Mind (3:08)/Crazy Love (3:31)/Haven't Met You Yet (4:04)/All I Do Is Dream Of You (2:32)/Hold On (4:05)/Heartache Tonight (3:52)/You're Nobody Till Somebody Loves You (3:07)/Baby (You've Got What It Takes) [feat. Sharon Jones & The Dap-Kings] (3:20)/At This Moment (4:35)/Stardust [feat. Naturally 7] (3:13)/Whatever It Takes [feat. Ron Sexsmith] (4:34)/Some Kind Of Wonderful (3:04)

CD2

Hollywood (4:13)/At This Moment (Live) (4:31)/Haven't Met You Yet (Live) (5:20)/End Of May (3:53)/Me And Mrs Jones (Live) (3:43)/Twist And Shout (Live) (1:52)/Heartache Tonight (Live) (3:46)/Best Of Me (4:33)

LIVE ALBUMS

Come Fly With Me
Released: March 8, 2004
Label: 143 / Reprise

Disc One (Audio CD)
Nice 'N' Easy/Can't Help Falling In Love/My Funny Valentine (Live)/Mack The Knife (Live)/Fever (Live)/You'll Never Know (Live)/For Once In My Life (Live)/Moondance (Live)

Disc Two (Live DVD)
Come Fly With Me/For Once In My Life/You'll Never Know/Kissing A Fool/Sway/Mack The Knife/That's All/Fever/How Can You Mend A Broken Heart/The Way You Look Tonight/Moondance/My Funny Valentine/The Way You Look Tonight (Sessions@AOL)/For Once In My Life (Sessions@AOL)/Kissing A Fool (Sessions@AOL)

Caught In The Act
Released: July 8, 2005
Label: 143 / Reprise

Disc One (Audio CD)
Feeling Good/Summer Wind/Home/You And I/The More I See You/You'll Never Find Another Love Like Mine [duet with Laura Pausini]/Can't Buy Me Love/Smile

Disc Two (DVD)
Feeling Good/Sway/Try A Little Tenderness/Fever/Come Fly With Me/Moondance/You Don't Know Me/That's All/For Once In My Life/You'll Never Find Another Love Like Mine [duet with Laura Pausini]/This Love/I've Got You Under My Skin/Home/The More I See You/Save The Last Dance For Me/

How Sweet It Is/Crazy Little Thing Called Love/A Song For You/A Song For You [duet with Chris Botti]

Michael Bublé Meets Madison Square Garden
Released: June 16, 2009
Label: 143 / Reprise

Disc One (Audio CD)
I'm Your Man/Me And Mrs Jones/Call Me Irresponsible/I've Got The World On A String/Lost/Feeling Good/Home/Everything/Crazy Little Thing Called Love/A Song For You

Fan Edition Bonus Tracks
Stardust/You're Nobody Till Somebody Loves You

Disc Two (DVD)
The DVD features 90 minutes of live performances, backstage footage and exclusive images.

INDEPENDENT RELEASES

First Dance (1996)
Learnin' The Blues (3.10)/I've Got You Under My Skin (3.36)/Just One More Dance (4.49)/All Of Me (2.17)/One Step At A Time (3.10)/I'll Be Seeing You (3.07)

BaBalu (2001)
Spider-Man Theme (3.01)/You Must Have Been A Beautiful Baby (2.43)/You'll Never Know (4.19)/Lazy River (4.17)/Oh Marie (2.47)/Can't Help Falling In Love (4.38)/Bill Bailey (3.12)/Buona Sera (3.45)/When You're Smiling (2.45)/What A Wonderful World (4.16)/Don't Get Around Much Anymore (2.31)/Mack The Knife (4.50)/La Vie En Rose (2.05)

Dream (2002)
Dream (3.43)/Anema E Cuore (3.29)/I'll Never Smile Again (3.46)/Stardust (5.13)/You Always Hurt The One You Love (3.31)/Don't Be A Baby, Baby (2.42)/Maria Elena (3.30)/Daddy's Little Girl (3.46)/Paper Doll (3.48)/Surrender (3.08)/Till Then (2.52)/You Belong To Me (2.47)/I Wish You Love (2.52)

Totally Bublé (2003)
That's How It Goes (2:25)/Peroxide Swing (2.38)/Me & Mrs You (2.06)/Love At First Sight (3:18)/Anyone To Love (2.06)/Guess I'm Falling 4 U (1.49)/Tell Him He's Yours (2.05)

SINGLES AND EPS

How Can You Mend A Broken Heart
Release date: February 4, 2003
Label: 143 Records, Reprise

How Can You Mend A Broken Heart (album version) (3:55)

Sway
Release date: June 22, 2004
Label: 143 Records, Reprise

Sway (Ralphi's Salsation edit)/Sway (Ralphi's Salsation vox)/Sway (Ralphi's dark rhumba dub)

Spider-Man Theme
Release date: July 4, 2004
Label: 143 Records, Reprise

Spider-Man Theme (Junkie XL remix)/Sway (Junkie XL remix)

Feeling Good
Release date: April 4, 2005
Label: 143 Records, Reprise

Feeling Good

Home
Release date: March 31, 2005
Label: 143 Records, Reprise

Home (radio mix with edit) (3:23)/Home (3:45)

Save The Last Dance For Me
Release date: April 4, 2006
Label: 143 Records, Reprise

Save The Last Dance For Me (3:38)/Save The Last Dance For Me (Ralphi's anthomic vocal) (9:36)/Save The Last Dance For Me (Ralphi's hydrolic dub) (8:29)

Everything
Release date: May 15, 2007
Label: 143 Records, Reprise

Everything (album version) (3:36)/These Foolish Things (Remind Me Of You) (4:48)/Everything (alternative mix) (3:30)

Let It Snow [EP]
Release date: October 16, 2007
Label: 143 Records, Reprise

Let It Snow/The Christmas Song/Grown-Up Christmas/I'll Be Home For Christmas/White Christmas/Let It Snow (Live)

Me and Mrs Jones
Release date: July 23, 2007
Label: 143 Records, Reprise

Me And Mrs Jones (album version) (4:33)

Lost
   Release date: October 1, 2007
   Label: 143 Records, Reprise

   Lost (album version) (3:40)/Lost (international pop mix) 3:27

It Had Better Be Tonight
   Release date: October 17, 2007
   Label: 143 Records, Reprise

   It Had Better Be Tonight (Meglio Stasera) (Eddie Amador club mix) (7:45)/It Had Better Be Tonight (Meglio Stasera) (Eddie Amador club dub) (5:15)/It Had Better Be Tonight (Meglio Stasera) (Eddie Amador's house lovers club) (8:04)/It Had Better Be Tonight (Meglio Stasera) (Eddie Amador's house lovers dub) (6:46)

Comin' Home Baby (with Boyz II Men)
   Release date: April 25, 2008
   Label: 143 Records, Reprise

Haven't Met You Yet
   Release date: August 31, 2009
   Label: 143 Records, Reprise

Digital Download
   Haven't Met You Yet (4:05)

The Remixes
   Haven't Met You Yet (Donni Hotwheel radio edit) (3:08)/Haven't Met You Yet (Donni Hotwheel extended) (4:35)/Haven't Met You Yet (Jason Nevins radio edit) (3:36)/Haven't Met You Yet (Jason Nevins club) (6:23)/Haven't Met You Yet (Cutmore club) (6:38)

Hold On
Release date: January 2010 (America), March 2011 (Worldwide)
Label: 143 Records, Reprise

Digital download
Hold On (4:05)/Miss This Feeling (4:12)

CD single
Hold On (JR Rotem mix) (3:51)/Hold On (Chris Lord Alge radio mix) (4:07)/Hold On (UK radio mix) (4:08)/Hold On (album version) (4:05)

Cry Me A River
Release date: March 15, 2010
Label: 143 Records, Reprise

Crazy Love
Release date: May 1, 2010
Label: 143 Records, Reprise

Hollywood
Release date: September 7, 2010
Label: 143 Records, Reprise

Digital Download (U.S.)
Hollywood (4:13)

European CD Single/Digital Download (U.K.)
Hollywood (4:13)/Mack The Knife (3:20)

Industry-Only Promo CD
Hollywood (radio edit) (3:35)/Hollywood (album version) (4:18)

Hollywood The Deluxe EP
Release date: October 25, 2010
Label: 143 Records, Reprise

Hollywood/At This Moment (Live)/Some Kind Of Wonderful/ End Of May/Me And Mrs Jones (Live)/Haven't Met You Yet (Live)/Heartache Tonight (Live)/Best Of Me